PROCEEDINGS

OF THE

Southern Commercial Convention,

AT ITS

ANNUAL SESSION

AT

CINCINNATI, OHIO, OCTOBER, 1870.

PUBLISHED BY THE
COMMITTEE OF ARRANGEMENTS OF CINCINNATI.

CINCINNATI:
1871.

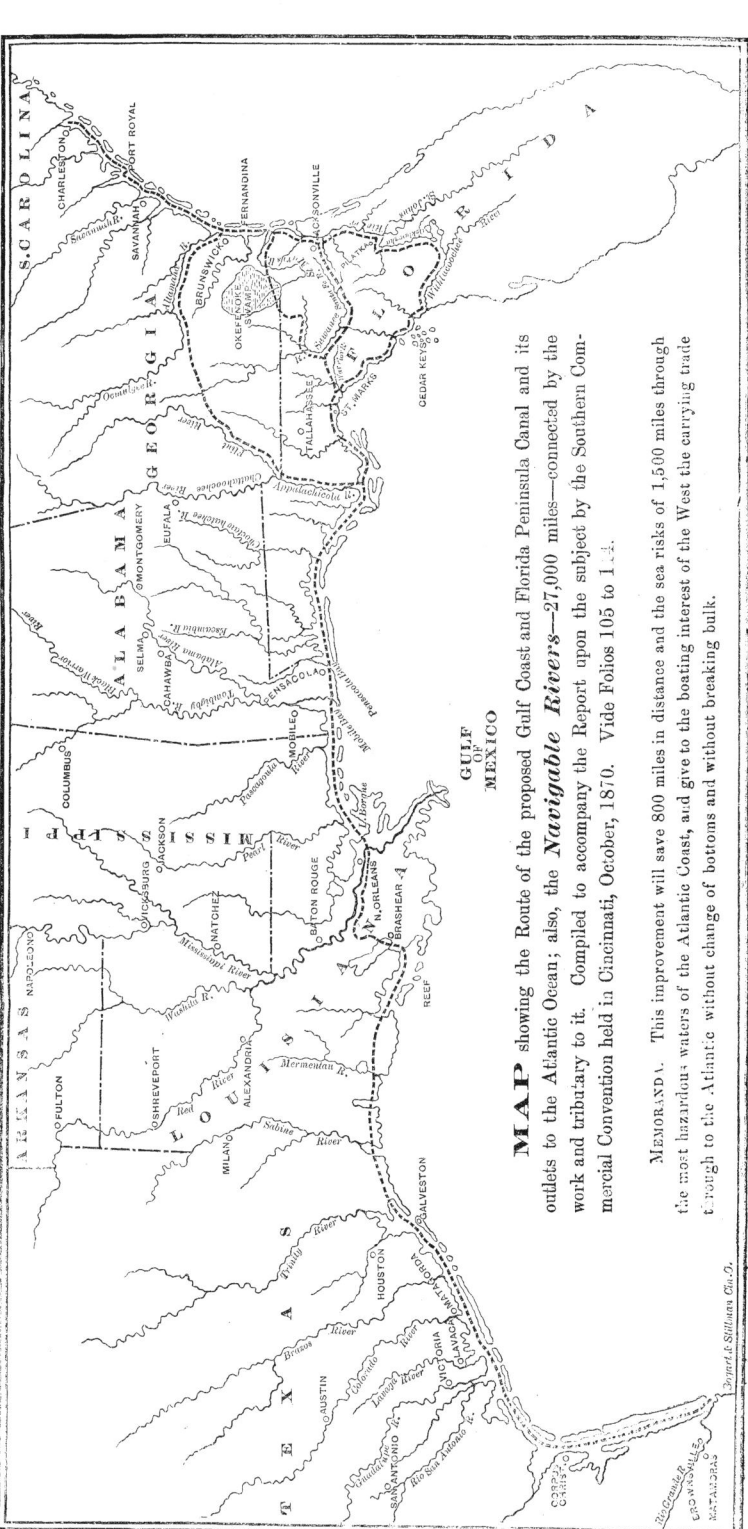

PROCEEDINGS

OF THE

Southern Commercial Convention,

AT ITS

ANNUAL SESSION

AT

CINCINNATI, OHIO, OCTOBER, 1870.

PUBLISHED BY THE
COMMITTEE OF ARRANGEMENTS OF CINCINNATI.

CINCINNATI:
1871.

RITCHIE & NEVINS, OFFICIAL STENOGRAPHERS,
49 West Third Street, Cincinnati, Ohio.

OFFICERS OF THE CONVENTION.

PRESIDENT.

Hon. JOHN W. GARRETT, Baltimore, Md.

VICE-PRESIDENTS.

Hon. M. D. WICKERSHAM	Alabama.
JOHN C. MACCABE	Arkansas.
Hon. R. B. HILTON	Florida.
Hon. R. L. MOTT	Georgia.
T. M. MONROE	Iowa.
J. W. PRESTON	Illinois.
Hon. WILLARD CARPENTER	Indiana.
JAMES BRIDGEFORD	Kentucky.
HIRAM S. SLEEPER	Kansas.
JOHN H. KENNARD	Louisiana.
E. STAFFORD	Mississippi.
Hon. R. C. HALLIDAY	Maryland.
Gov. E. O. STANNARD	Missouri.
JAMES J. NEWALL	Michigan.
Hon. NATHANIEL P. BANKS	Massachusetts.
BENJ. P. BAKER	New York.
JOHN G. FOX	Nevada.
J. C. MILLS	North Carolina.
Gov. A. G. McBURNEY	Ohio.
JAMES S. GIBBONS	Pennsylvania.
WILLIAM S. HASTIE	South Carolina.
Hon. M. BURNS	Tennessee.
Gov. G. W. THROCKMORTON	Texas.
JOSEPH R. ANDERSON	Virginia.
BREESE J. STEVENS	Wisconsin.

SECRETARIES.

H. H. TATEM	Cincinnati, O.
WILLIAM R. BOWES	Michigan City, Ind.
ALBERT W. MULLEN	Cincinnati, O.
WILLIAM T. PERKINS	Cincinnati, O.
JOHN J. HENDERSON	Cincinnati, O.

READING CLERK.

JULIUS F. BLACKBURN .... Cincinnati, O.

PROCEEDINGS OF THE CONVENTION.

FIRST DAY.

CINCINNATI, Ohio, October 4th, 1870.

The Southern Commercial Convention having assembled at 11 o'clock, A. M., in Pike's Music Hall, it was called to order by Hon. R. M. BISHOP, of Ohio, Vice President of the Convention held at Louisville, Ky., in October, 1869.

Mr. BISHOP said:

GENTLEMEN OF THE CONVENTION:

In the absence of the Hon. MILLARD FILLMORE, President of the late Southern Commercial Convention, at Louisville, as a Vice President of that Convention, from the State of Ohio, I have been requested by the Committee of Arrangements to call this Convention to order. The task which has been imposed upon me is a pleasant one. It is exceedingly pleasant to me to meet my fellow countrymen, from nearly all the States of this Union, who have been sent here, and who have met together for the purpose of deliberating upon important subjects in which we are all directly interested. That our deliberations may be such as they should be, we will now, if the audience will please to arise, invoke the divine blessing.

The delegates arose, and Rev. J. L. ROBERTSON made a prayer.

Mr. R. M. BISHOP: Gentlemen, I now have the pleasure of introducing Hon. GEORGE F. DAVIS, President of the Board of Aldermen of Cincinnati, who will deliver a few words of salutation on behalf of our city government. (Applause.)

Mr. DAVIS came forward on the platform and spoke as follows:

MR. CHAIRMAN AND GENTLEMEN OF THE SOUTHERN COMMERCIAL CONVENTION:

It is made my pleasant duty, on behalf of the city government of Cincinnati, in the absence of his Honor the Mayor, to welcome you to our city. I do this the more heartily because you do not come to seek your own good as individuals, or that of any particular locality, but to consider the best interests of our whole country. Four meetings at Memphis, New Orleans and Louisville—the two first of which I had the pleasure of attending—were productive of much good, not only in the consideration of great commercial questions, but in the formation of acquaintances among ourselves; to a better knowledge of the necessities of the various portions of the country, and of their competence and ability, under a wise administration of affairs, to remedy them. We welcome you here, because we desire to form social acquaintance with you. Our country is so extended that we have need to come together in some sort of annual gathering, that we may gather up and carry back to the remote sections of our land the good will of each. Trade is said to be selfish; but with its twin sister, commerce, it has been the forerunner of that which has been for the greatest good of mankind, the promotion of civil and religious liberty. Therefore, we welcome you as the representatives of the best interests of our whole country, and controlling that which by proper guidance, may keep this great aggregation of commonwealths united in one common bond of union. Last year you met in a sister State, united by her Virginia mother to the Atlantic ocean on the east, and by the Mississippi and its tributaries to the north-west, west and south to the great gulf of Mexico. To-day, you meet again on the border, in a State not less noble, and also united on the north, and thence east and west, by the noblest chain of lakes in the world, and by her river to the same great south and west as her sister State of Kentucky. Isolate either of these commonwealths from each other and the rest of the country, and what harm to themselves, and what confusion to all others concerned! How can a land so united as we are by river and lake, by history and language and social ties, be disunited? May we not hope that these meetings on the border may be the means of uniting us all in one. We welcome you, therefore, with high hopes and large anticipations, that the results of your deliberations may result in great good to our common country. And now, gentlemen of the Convention, I have the further pleasure of announcing that the people of our city are desirous of extending you a cordial welcome, and have chosen a distinguished son of Ohio to speak in their behalf. I have the honor of introducing to you the Hon. GEORGE H. PENDLETON.

Mr. PENDLETON was received with prolonged and enthusiastic cheers by the Convention. After some moments, silence was restored, and Mr. PENDLETON spoke as follows:

GENTLEMEN OF THE CONVENTION:

My fellow citizens have done me infinite honor to-day. The civic authorities, the commercial authorities, the Chamber of Commerce, the Board of Trade, the people generally, have commissioned me to speak to you in their behalf.

They have commanded me to give you a most fraternal greeting. They have commanded me to say, with a sincerity and warmth for which I find no fitting words, that you are their honored and most welcome guests. They have commanded me to say that they appreciate the honor of your presence here, and they desire to recognize it by every act of courteous, and attentive, and affectionate hospitality. (Applause.)

These annually recurring meetings—this concourse of representative men—these delegations from every State and City and Chamber of Commerce and combination of business men, from the Hudson to the Rio Grande—these earnest, thoughtful, learned debates by friends of every industrial interest, and advocates of every growing enterprise, from the Alleghanies to the Rocky mountains—attest the dignity of this Convention, and the magnitude of the questions committed to its consideration.

Your predecessors who met at Norfolk in 1868 were few in numbers, and the chief subject of their consideration was the ocean trade of the Atlantic cities with Europe.

Your numbers already reach many hundreds; and your debates will touch every project of material development—every phase of intelligent industry—every facility of commercial intercourse—every plan of finance and taxation—every encouragement of immigration—every question of governmental economy.

It must be so. This Convention meets to consider and advance the interests of the great Mississippi valley. I say this in no selfish or sectional sense. I say it in no narrow spirit. I would limit your duties and your influence to no local lines.

The interests of the Mississippi valley are the center and source of the well being of other portions of the country. Its development is their growth. Its prosperity is their wealth; and when the hand of industry touches into life any dormant element of power which nature has hidden in its fields, or mines, or lakes, or rivers, they grow by its activity, and move under its impulsion.

The Mississippi valley! The very name calls up a vision of transcendent grandeur. Mountains filled with ores; valleys instinct with fecund life; prairies carpeted with the most brilliant wild flowers, and redolent of the sweetest perfumes; lands generous with wheat, corn and barley; lands teeming with cotton, rice and sugar; the snow-clad fields of the North shading into the dusky yellow of the parched and thirsty South; the freezing blasts of Canada, melted to genial breezes in the warm embrace of the fervent winds of Florida.

It stretches from central Pennsylvania to the western boundary of Kansas, from the Lake of the Woods to the gulf of Mexico. Its soils are fertile; its mines are productive; its forests are exhaustless; its skies are bright; its climates are healthful; God has given to it every element of wealth; every attribute of beauty; and through its whole length the great river, made of the confluent waters of every spring and rivulet and stream in all its broad expanse, rolls its ceaseless flood from the frozen regions of the arctic ices to the golden orange groves of the sun-begotten tropics.

Cheap lands and abounding breadstuffs will secure its future. Ere long a hundred millions of people will inhabit it. They will till its fertile soil; they will work its fruitful mines; they will manufacture its raw materials; they will bring every force of nature into co-operation with every appliance of art, and use both with every device of human ingenuity and every effort of human industry in the development of its unrivaled resources.

They will be an active, enterprising, self-reliant, audacious people.

They will not submit to isolation.

They will require and they will have free, uninterrupted, easy communication with the gulf of Mexico by the Mississippi river; with the Chesapeake by the canals of Virginia; with Sandy Hook by the canals of New York; with the North Atlantic by the lakes and the St. Lawrence.

They will reach the Pacific by the Northern and the Central and the Southern Railroads.

They will dig through the mountains of Virginia, and import by way of Norfolk. They will thread the valleys of Kentucky and Tennessee, and load the ships of Charleston and Savannah. They will build the levees of the southern rivers, and reclaim to cultivation their rich alluvion.

They will sweep away every embarrassment, caused by a restrictive, or, if you prefer the word, a protective system; and they will demand every improvement in the burden of taxation and in the benefits of currency which the most enlightened and sagacious civilization can suggest.

And I would fain believe that in the midst of this splendid material advancement they will never forget that in the eyes of God and humanity they are charged with the preservation of free government, and with the maintenance, as its best guarantee, of the confederated system of our fathers. (Loud applause.)

Does this consummation seem improbable?

Look at the ocean telegraph, at the Pacific railroad, at the Suez canal, at the delicate machinery which does actually supply the place of human hands, and can almost think! and who shall doubt that the Almighty has touched with living fire the inventive genius of this age, and has subjugated to the control of daring and audacious man the mysterious forces which fill the earth, and sea, and air.

"We live in deeds, not in years; in thought, not breaths;
In feelings, not in figures on the dial.
We should count time by heart throbs;
He most lives
Who thinks most, feels noblest, acts the best."

Gentlemen, it is your work to aid this development—to set in motion those agencies which shall tend to its accomplishment.

This is the Southern Commercial Convention.

Ohio was the first fruit of the munificence of liberal, patriotic, magnanimous Virginia. Eldest-born of the north-west, the fairest of her sisters, conscious of her own matured and matronly beauty, she looks with loving pride upon their youthful bloom and vigor. In her name I bid you welcome.

Cincinnati is the queen of the Ohio. She has been throned by her industry; and the dark crown which sits forever upon her fair brow is the symbol of her royalty and the sign of her intelligent and indomitable labor. In her name I bid you welcome!

Her people are sagacious enough to be foresighted, wise enough to be instructed, large enough to take within their affections every one of their countrymen.

In their names I bid you welcome, thrice welcome, to their homes and their hearthstones!

Wild applause followed the conclusion of Mr. PENDLETON's address.

Mr. THEODORE COOK, Chairman of the Committee of Arrangements, then announced to the Convention that as soon as the number of delegates from each State had been reported to the Secretary, arrangements would be made to have the members of each delegation located together, and requested the chairman of each State delegation to report as soon as possible. Mr. COOK also announced the place selected for headquarters of the Convention, and where the committee rooms were located. Also, that the Committee of Arrangements proposed to have a Banquet on Friday evening, and requested that delegates would make no other arrangements for that evening.

Mr. COOK then read notes of invitation to the delegates from the Y. M. M. Library Association; from the managers of the Industrial Exposition; from the Managers of the Theaters; from the President of the Street R. R. Companies; from the President of the Chamber of Commerce; from the Managers of the Telegraph Lines, and followed these with the reading of the official list of subjects submitted for the consideration of the Convention, as follows:

The following subjects having been officially reported to the Committee of Arrangements are presented to this Convention for its consideration and action:

1. Direct trade between southern Atlantic cities and Europe.—(Adjourned from Louisville Convention.)
2. Southern Pacific Railroad.—(Adjourned from Louisville Convention.)
3. Obstruction to navigation by narrow span bridge piers.—(Adjourned from Louisville Convention.)
4. Continuous water line communication between the Mississippi river and the Atlantic seaboard.—(Adjourned from Louisville Convention.)
5. Removal of obstructions from the mouth of the Mississippi river.—(Adjourned from Louisville Convention.)
6. Construction of permanent levees on the Mississippi river.—(Adjourned from Louisville Convention.)
7. Finance and taxation.—(Adjourned from Louisville Convention.)
8. Removal of the national capitol.—(From St. Louis.)
9. To abolish all toll charges on the navigable rivers of the United States.—(From Cincinnati Board of Trade.)
10. The enlargement of the more important lines of canal in the United States so as to render them navigable for vessels propelled by steam.—(From Cincinnati.)
11. The charges on passenger and freight traffic by rail and water lines.—(From Cincinnati Board of Trade.)
12. That all railway viaducts over navigable rivers, be made highways for railroad companies, which will pay their pro-rata toll on same; and that efforts be made to secure legislation to that effect.—(From Cincinnati Chamber Commerce.)
13. To abolish throughout the whole country all license imposed on commercial travelers.—(Cincinnati Board of Trade.)
14. Free trade in money.—(Cincinnati Chamber of Commerce.)
15. A settled policy in the public interest in regard to the disposition of the Government lands.—(City of Cincinnati.)
16. Improvement of seacoast harbors.—(From Mobile Board of Trade.)
17. Wharfage on the navigable rivers.—(City of St. Louis.)
18. Ample railroad facilities from the Ohio river to the central south.—(From Chattanooga, Tenn.)
19. Direct and reciprocal trade with Brazil and other South American countries.—(From Dubuque, Iowa.)
20. Tares and short weights.—(From Cincinnati Chamber of Commerce.)

RESOLUTION ADOPTED AT SESSION OF SOUTHERN COMMERCIAL CONVENTION, HELD AT LOUISVILLE, KY., OCTOBER 12TH, 1869.

Resolved, That the regular Standing Committees of the Louisville Convention, be requested to report for the respectful consideration of the next Commercial Convention upon the subject for which said Committees were respectively raised, and that the Chairman of said regular Committees be *ipso facto* members of said next Convention.

Mr. COOK from the Committee of Arrangements also stated that interesting letters, some of which referred to the subjects before the Convention, had been received from the following named gentlemen:

B. F. Potts, Governor of Montana; David J. Burr, Richmond, Virginia; Wm. Preston Johnston, Lexington, Virginia; Edward Young, Chief United States Bureau of Statistics; John L. Chamberlain, Governor of Maine; Hamilton A. Hill, Secretary and Treasurer National Board of Trade, Boston; Frederick Fraley, Philadelphia, President National Board of Trade; A. McDonald, Arkansas; Governor J. W. Stevenson, Kentucky; Senator Howard, Michigan; Bellamy Storer, William Dennison, Columbus; F. A. Sawyer, New York; R. Ransom, Wilmington, North Carolina; T. W. Ashborn, Jacksonville, Florida; F. O. Howe, Michigan; Governor Powell Clayton, Arkansas; Wendell Phillips; James Longstreet, New Orleans; General George B. McClellan; Governor David Butler, Nebraska; Aaron F. Perry, Cincinnati; Alphonso Taft, Ex-President Millard Fillmore, Senator John Sherman, Hon. Hamilton Fish, Carl Schurz; George Vickers, Maryland; Henry A. Wise, Virginia; George W. H. Smith, Alabama; Postmaster General Creswell; Josiah Quincy, Massachusetts; Governor J. W. McClurg, Missouri; Commodore Maury, Virginia; R. D. Bullock, Georgia; Senator Willard Warner, Alabama; Senator Ramsey, Minnesota; Governor Padelford, Rhode Island; W. S. Groesbeck, Cincinnati; Horace Capron, Washington, D. C.

Which were ordered given to the press for publication.

On motion, a committee of one from each State, on permanent organization, on rules and order of business, and on credentials was ordered,—the Chairman of each State delegation to name a gentleman for each of the Committees, as the roll of States is called by the Secretary.

A recess of fifteen minutes was then taken, after which the Convention was called to order by Mr. BISHOP, the Chairman, and the Secretary called the States with the following result:

COMMITTEE ON PERMANENT ORGANIZATION.

Alabama, G. H. Wilcox; Arkansas, Geo. E. Dodge; Florida, H. L. Hart; Georgia, H. D. Capers; Iowa, T. M. Monroe; Indiana, F. P. Carson; Kentucky, S. W. Morton; Kansas, W. G. Coffin; Louisiana, C. F. Buddeke; Mississippi, C. A. Foster; Maryland, R. R. Kirkland; Missouri, Barton Able; Michigan, J. J. Newell; Massachusetts, R. E. Robbins; New York, J. H. Drake; Nevada, John G. Fox; North Carolina, J. C. Mills; Ohio, Judge O'Brien; South Carolina, W. S. Hastie; Tennessee, Wm. J. Sykes; Texas, C. G. Forshey; Virginia, W. W. Walker; Wisconsin, D. M. Kelley; Illinois, P. W. Dater.

COMMITTEE ON ORDER OF BUSINESS.

Alabama, Charles A. Miller; Arkansas, B. D. Williams; Florida, P. H. Raiford; Georgia, B. A. Gaskill; Iowa, H. W. Rothert; Indiana, H. W. Cloud; Kentucky, Charles R. Long; Kansas, J. L. Pendery; Louisiana, D. C. LaBatt; Mississippi, J. P. Pryor; Maryland, S. P. Thompson; Missouri, D. T. Jewett; Michigan, J. J. Jewell; Massachusetts, N. P. Banks; New York, P. Clark; Nevada, J. G. Fox; North Carolina, J. C. Mills; Ohio, B. F. Eggleston; South Carolina, J. Barrett Cohen; Tennessee, D. A. Kennedy; Texas, G. W. Throckmorton; Virginia, John E. Roller; Wisconsin, B. J. Stevens; Illinois, O. S. Hough.

COMMITTEE ON CREDENTIALS.

Alabama, J. M. Humphrey; Arkansas, J. C. Maccabe; Florida, R. B. Hilton; Georgia, W. W. Fluellen; Iowa, T. M. Munroe; Indiana, S. E. Gilbert; Kentucky, A. S. Berry; Kansas, Isaac Young; Louisiana, J. W. Sherer; Mississippi, T. W. Stringer; Maryland, Robert Fowler; Missouri, Clinton B. Fisk; Michigan, J. J. Newell; Massachusetts, N. P. Banks; New York, J. R. Turner; Nevada, J. G. Fox; North Carolina, A. A. Campbell; Ohio, C. W. Rowland; South Carolina, George L. Holmes; Tennessee, W. P. Rathbourn; Texas, A. C. McKeehan; Virginia, R. D. Lilley; Wisconsin, O. B. Thomas; Illinois, P. L. Underwood.

The Convention then adjourned until three o'clock, P. M.

AFTERNOON SESSION.

The Convention met at three o'clock, P. M. Mr. R. M. BISHOP in the chair.

The CHAIRMAN: Gentlemen, the first business in order will be the reports of Committees, commencing with the report of the Committee on Credentials.

Gen. N. P. BANKS, Chairman of the Committee on Credentials, then made the following report:

CINCINNATI, October 4th, 1870.

The Committee to which was referred the credentials of delegates to the Convention, with instructions to examine and report upon the same, have attended to the duty assigned to the Committee, and respectfully report, that delegates properly accredited are present from twenty-five States, viz: Alabama, Arkansas, Florida, Georgia, Iowa, Illinois, Indiana, Kentucky, Kansas, Louisiana, Mississippi, Maryland, Missouri, Michigan; Massachusetts, New York, Nevada, North Carolina, Ohio, Pennsylvania, South Carolina, Tennessee, Texas, Virginia and Wisconsin, and also from (75) seventy five of the principal cities, representing the commercial interests of the United States. That the number of delegates now present is (350) three hundred and fifty, all of whom are properly accredited and entitled to seats as members of the Convention, for the States and cities they are appointed to represent—a list of delegates is herewith appended:

NAMES OF DELEGATES.	REPRESENTING.	CITIES.
Armistead, Jno C	City	Petersburg, Va.
Alexander, Hon. Jno	City	Columbia, S. C.
Allen, Hon. Jas. L	State	Danville, Ky.
Applegate, Wm. A	City	Cincinnati, O.
Adams, Capt. M. B	Webster's f'dy. & mach. w.	Chattanooga, Tenn.
Able, Capt. Barton	Union Merch. Ex	St. Louis, Mo.
Ainsley, Geo	City	Louisville, Ky.
Armel, Wm	City	Cincinnati, O.
Alloway, N. E	City	Nashville, Tenn.
Anderson, Gen. Jos. R	Cham. of Com	Richmond, Va.
Archer, Wm. M	City	Richmond, Va.
Addy, Mathew	City	Cincinnati, O.
Burch, Hon. J. C	City	Nashville, Tenn.
Bishop, R. M	Board of Trade	Cincinnati, O.
Burns, M	5th Tenn. Cong. District	Nashville, Tenn.
Brien, W. G	City	Nashville, Tenn.

SOUTHERN COMMERCIAL CONVENTION. 15

NAMES OF DELEGATES.	REPRESENTING.	CITIES.
Bass, Col. Jno M	City	Nashville, Tenn.
Bryson, Col. M. A	U. M. Exchange	St. Louis, Mo.
Blackman, A. O	U. M. Exchange	St. Louis, Mo.
Brinkley, J B	City	Baltimore, Md.
Brinkley, Hon. Jos. P	State	Baltimore, Md.
Blumenberg, Gen. L	City	Baltimore, Md.
Beckurts, Herm	City	Louisville, Ky.
Bishop, Harry	City	Louisville, Ky.
Bridgeford, Jas	City	Louisville, Ky.
Bradey, D C	Board of Trade	Louisville, Ky.
Barkhouse, L	Board of Trade	Louisville, Ky.
Burch, Geo	Southern Stock Yards	Louisville, Ky.
Baldwin, Frank H	City	Cincinnati, O.
Barr, L T	City	Cincinnati, O.
Boaz, W. T	City	Cincinnati, O.
Bare, Martin	City	Cincinnati, O.
Burton, Gideon	City	Cincinnati, O.
Butler, Jos. C	State	Cincinnati, O.
Biggs, Hon. Thos. R	Cham. of Com	Cincinnati, O.
Bruce, W. S	City	Memphis, Tenn.
Bates, Jas. H	State	Memphis, Tenn.
Buddecke, C. T	Cham. of Com	New Orleans, La.
Baker, Marion A	City	New Orleans, La.
Burwell, W. M	City	New Orleans, La.
Baker, O. R	Cham. of Com	New York City.
Baker, Col. Ben. P	New York Cotton Ex	New York City.
Barkesdale, Capt. H	City	Jackson, Miss.
Brown, Isaac	Star Furnace Co	Jackson, O.
Bowen, Judge O	State	Marion, O.
Branham, J. Jr	Etna Iron Co	Rome, Ga.
Banks, Nath. P. Gov	State	Waltham, Mass.
Barbour, B. J	Tred Iron Works	Gordonsville, Va.
Baum, Col. L. S	C. & V. W. R. R. Co	Atlanta, Ga.
Berry, A. S	State	Newport, Ky.
Bowman, J. B	Regent Ky. University	Lexington, Ky.
Berry, Austin	State	Zanesville, O.
Baldwin, H. F	State	Toledo, O.
Boles, Col. W. M	Union Iron Co	Portsmouth, O.
Bowes, W. R	City	Michigan City, Ind.
Behan, W. J	State	New Orleans, La.
Buck, Hon. R. C	City	Vicksburg, Miss.
Branch, Col. Thos	State	Richmond, Va.
Breed, G. C	M., C. & L. R. R	Clarksville, Tenn.
Butler, Wm. A	City	Detroit, Mich.
Bishop, Levi	City	Detroit, Mich.
Broome, J. R	Rock Mills Manuf. Co	Rock Mills, Ala.
Burroughs, Dr. R. B	City	Tallahassee, Fla.
Butsch, Val	City	Indianapolis, Ind.
Buell, Gen. Geo. P	State	Waco, Tex.
Button, Chas. W	City	Lynchburg, Va.
Carson, Capt. F. P	City	Evansville, Ind.
Cloud, Dr. H. W	City	Evansville, Ind.
Carpenter, William	City	Evansville, Ind.
Chilton, Gen. Geo. W	State at Large	Louisville, Ky.

SOUTHERN COMMERCIAL CONVENTION.

NAMES OF DELEGATES.	REPRESENTING.	CITIES.
Crutcher, Dr. Jas	State	New Castle, Ky.
Crach, J. A	City	Louisville, Ky.
Cubbins, Jno	State	Memphis, Tenn.
Church, Capt. C. B	City	Memphis, Tenn.
Clapp, J. W	City	Memphis, Tenn.
Cole, E. W	Nash. & Chattanooga R. R.	Nashville, Tenn.
Clark, M. H	Board of Trade	Clarksville, Tenn.
Coulter, M. B	Chat. Leath Manf. Co.	Chattanoogo, Tenn.
Cook, Theodore	Board of Trade	Cincinnati, O.
Clough, H. P	Cham. of Com.	Cincinnati, O.
Carrothers, Wm. H	Globe Rolling Mill Co	Cincinnati, O.
Corwine, Hon. R. M	City	Cincinnati, O.
Clark, Jas. M	City	Cincinnati, O.
Chamberlain, S	State	Columbus, O.
Cohen, J. Barrett	Cham. of Com	Charleston, S. C.
Carrington, I. H	Cham. of Com	Richmond, Va.
Clark, Peter	M. & O. S. N. Co	New York City.
Camp, C. B	Cotton Exchange	New York City.
Coffin, Col. W. G	City	Leavenworth, Kansas.
Capers, Col. H. D	State	Savannah, Ga.
Cantwell, Dr. J. Y	City	Decatur, Ala.
Clark, Maj. P. G	State	Mobile, Ala.
Cheever, H. M	City	Mobile, Ala.
Casey, Jas. B	City	Covington, Ky.
Carlisle, Hon. Jno. G	City	Covington, Ky.
Cutcheon, Hon. S. M	State	Detroit, Mich.
Carter, Dr. Jno	City	New Orleans, La.
Clark, Chas. A	City	Rodney, Miss.
Campbell, A. A	Tomotla Iron Co	North Carolina.
Dale, Jno. P	City	Nashville, Tenn.
Danbury, J. D	City	Memphis, Tenn.
Dallan, Wm. W	City	Baltimore, Md.
Davis, Jno. B	City	Louisville, Ky.
Dorn, Julius	Board of Trade	Louisville, Ky.
Dater, P. W	Board of Trade	Chicago, Ills.
Dixon, Arthur	City	Chicago, Ills.
Darnell, S. H	ty	Jasper, Ga.
Dorsey, Hon. J. V	State	Piqua, Ohio.
Dodge, Geo. E	State	Little Rock, Ark.
Dravo, Capt. Chas. A	State	Pittsburg, Pa.
Drake, Jas. H	Produce Exchange	New York City.
Eggleston, Hon. B	Cham. of Com	Cincinnati, O.
Elliott, R. S	Union Merch. Ex	St. Louis, Mo.
Edwards, Richard	City	St. Louis, Mo.
Emley, S. C	City	New Orleans, La.
Enders, Jno	City	Richmond, Va.
Ernst, Wm	State	Covington, Ky.
Fisk, Gen. C. B	Union Merch. Ex	St. Louis, Mo.
Fletcher, Hon. T. C	Union Merch. Ex	St. Louis, Mo.
Forshey, Col. C. G	Cham. of Com	Galveston, Tex.
Fox, Jno. G	State of Nevada	Carson City, Nevada.
Fearing, Gen. B. D	Blymyer, Norton & Co	Cincinnati, O.

SOUTHERN COMMERCIAL CONVENTION. 17

NAMES OF DELEGATES.	REPRESENTING.	CITIES.
Fowler, Hon. J. S	Hon. Delegate	Nashville, Tenn.
Fowler, Hon. Robert	State	Baltimore, Md.
Fowler, Robert S	City	Baltimore, Md.
Fluellen, Dr. W. W	City	Columbus, Ga.
Fisher, Harry	City	Baltimore, Md.
Foster, Hon. C. A	State	Vicksburg, Miss.
Fellows, E. T	City	New Orleans, La.
Garrett, Hon. Jno. W	City and State	Baltimore, Md.
Garrett, Robert	City	Baltimore, Md.
George, I S	City	Baltimor, Md.
Gracey, F. P	City	Clarksville, Tenn.
Greenwood, Miles	Board of Trade	Cincinnati, O.
Glassford, H. A	Board of Trade	Cincinnati, O.
Glenn, Jas M	Cham. of Com	Cincinnati, O.
Gano, Gazzam	City	Cincinnati, O.
Gilpin, Thos	City	Cincinnati, O.
George, Jno. D	City	Griffin, Ga.
Gaskill, Hon. B. A	State	Atlanta, Ga.
Gibbons, Jas. S	State	Philadelphia, Pa.
Gilbert, Samuel E	City	Evansville, Ind.
Grubbs, Jno. W	City	Richmond, Ind.
Glasgow, I. I	City	Richmond, Va.
Gibson, Jas. W	Cham. of Com	Richmond, Va.
Greaner, Jno. H	City	Richmond, Va.
Geisler, Hon. Samuel	City	Newport, Ky.
Graham, Andrew	Board of Trade	Louisville, Ky.
German, Phil. T	Board of Trade	Louisville, Ky.
Gregg, Geo. W	State	Circleville, O.
Gastrell, H. M	City	Natchez, Miss.
Gwyn, Samuel	Cotton Exchange	New York City.
Hill, Dr. J. C	Washington & O. R. R	Alexandria, Va.
Hughes, Robert W	V., & R. R. R	Lynchburg, Va.
Hilton, Hon. R. B	City	Tallahassee, Fla.
Hart, H. L	W. & P. can. & steam bt. Co	Palatka, Fla.
Hollyday, Hon. C	State	Annapolis, Md.
Hotchkiss, T. P	City	Shreveport, La.
Hancock, E. C	City	New Orleans, La.
Higby, L. J	City	New Orleans, La.
Higby, L. J	Cham. of Com	New Orleans, La.
Humphrey, Gen. Jno. M	City	Huntsville, Ala.
Hamilton, Hon. P	Board of Trade	Mobile, Ala
Holmes, Geo. L	Board of Trade	Charleston, S. C.
Hastie, Wm. S	Board of Trade	Charleston, S. C.
Huntington, H. D	C., H. & D. R. R	Cincinnati, O.
Hord, Geo. M	City	Cincinnati, O.
Hull, Leverett R	City	Cincinnati, O.
Hudson, Homer	City	Covington, Ky.
Honshell, Col. D. S	L. & Big Sandy R. R	Newport, Ky.
Hough, O. S	Board of Trade	Chicago, Ills.
Holden, Chas. C. P	City	Chicago, Ills.
Harris, Dr. J. J	City	Brunswick, Ga.
Huntley, Wm. H	City	LaGrange, Ga.
Hutchins, B. T	New Era & A. Ga. Daily	Atlanta, Ga.

18   SOUTHERN COMMERCIAL CONVENTION.

NAMES OF DELEGATES.	REPRESENTING.	CITIES.
Hawley, Hon. Richard	City	Detroit, Mich.
Hartwell, Thos. H	City	Detroit, Mich.
James, Hon. E. A	Chmn. Com. Tenn. R. Imp.	Chattanooga, Tenn.
Jones, Hon. Thos. M	Nash. & Decatur R. R.	Pulaski, Tenn.
Johnson, M. H	City	Clarksville, Tenn.
Johnson, Geo. L	Board of Trade	Cincinnati, O.
Johnson, T. S	Cham. of Com	Cincinnati, O.
Jewett, Hon. D. T	State	St. Louis, Mo.
Jewett, G. M	L., A. & N. W. R. R	Leavenworth, Kansas.
Jonas, M. B	City	Mobile, Ala.
Kennard, John H	City	New Orleans, La.
Kerr, Capt. James	Kouns Line Red Riv. Stmrs	New Orleans, La.
Kirkland, Robt. R	Board of Trade and City	Baltimore, Md.
Kaiser, H. I	City	Baltimore, Md.
Keene, Edw. A	City	Baltimore, Md.
Kennedy, D. A	State	Clarksville, Tenn.
Kelly, D. M	State	Greensburg, Wis.
Kinsey, Joseph	City	Cincinnati, O.
Lane, P. P	Hon. Delegate	Cincinnati, O.
Lippencott, W. J	Cham. of Com	Cincinnati, O.
Lye, F. J., Jr	State	Delphos, O.
Little, Hon. W. W	City	Portsmouth, O.
Lowry, J. J	Vulcan Iron Works	Chattanooga, Tenn.
Laurey, H. Z	Cham. of Com	Charleston, S. C.
Lilley, Gen. R. D	Washington Coll., Va	Lexington, Va.
Long, Chas. R	City	Louisville, Ky.
Labatt, David C	City	New Orleans, La.
Miller, Saml. A	City	Louisville, Ky.
Moss, Henry	City	Louisville, Ky.
Montgomery, Jos	City	Louisville, Ky.
Merriweather, W. H	City	Louisville. Ky.
McCollough, A. D	City	Louisville, Ky.
McIlvain, Jno. B	Manuf. & Finance Co	Louisville, Ky.
Morton, S. W	State	Lexington, Ky.
Mitchell, Robert	Mitchell & R. Fur. Co	Cincinnati, O.
Mathers, Richard	Cham. of Com	Cincinnati, O.
McLean, Gen. N. C	City & Del. of Post & Co.	Cincinnati, O.
Macready, R	City	Cincinnati, O.
Minor, Jno. D	City	Cincinnati, O.
Moerlein, Chris	City	Cincinnati, O.
Matthews, Hon. S	City	Cincinnati, O.
Mills, Jos. F	Cham. of Com	Cincinnati, O.
McBurney, A. G	State	Lebanon, O.
McClintick, W T	M. & C. R. R	Chillicothe, O.
McKaig. T. J., Jr	City	Baltimore, Md.
Mules, T. H	City	Baltimore, Md.
Mott, Hon. R. L	3d Georgia Con. Dist	Columbus, Ga.
McCany, Col. S. R	City	Atlanta, Ga.
Moore, Hon. M. M	State	Savannah, Ga.
Munroe, T. M	Chn. Com. on Cen. Wtr. Line	Dubuque, Iowa.
Maccabe, J. C	1st Ark. Con. Dist	Helena, Ark.

SOUTHERN COMMERCIAL CONVENTION. 19

NAMES OF DELEGATES.	REPRESENTING.	CITIES.
Mills, J. C	Board of Trade	Charlotte, N. C.
Miller, Col. C. A	State	Montgomery, Ala.
Miller, Hon. Wm	City	Mobile, Ala.
Mayer, L. H	City	Mobile, Ala.
Meek, R	M. C. & L. R. R	Clarksville, Tenn.
Moore, Hon. W. D	City	Pittsburg, Pa.
Maney, George	State	Tennessee.
Martin, Prof. Chas	State	Ham. Sid. College.
McCanley, Hon. Jas	City	Chicago, Ills
Mihills, U. D	State	Fond du Lac, Wis.
Newman, W. T	A. & R. Air L. R. R	Atlanta, Ga.
Noble, James	Rome Iron Works	Rome, Ga.
Noyes, D. J. O	State & City	New Orleans, La.
Nagle, J. E	New Orleans Press	New Orleans, La.
Newall, Jas. J	City	Adrian, Mich.
Newton, Dr. R. S	M. & O. Steam Nav. Co	New York.
Newland, Dr. E	City	New Albany, Ind.
O'Neil, Bern	Board of Trade	Charleston, S. C.
Osborne, R C	City	Petersburg, Va.
Overall, E. E	City	Oxford, Miss.
Pittman, Hon. Danl	City	Atlanta, Ga.
Pitner, A. G	Rome R. R. Co	Rome, Ga.
Powell, Nathaniel	City	Madison, Ind.
Pierce, Hon. W. S	City	Indianapolis, Ind.
Purcell, Hon. James	6th Cong. Dist	Washington C H., O.
Pierson, Danl. B	Mil. Lumber Co	Cincinnati, O.
Potts, Edward	City	Baltimore, Md.
Pryor, Col. J. P	City	Corinth, Miss.
Prescott, G. P	City	Richmond, Va.
Prague, F. A	City	Covington, Ky.
Park, Howard P	City	Opelika, Ala.
Pendery, Hon. J. L	Board of Trade	Leavenworth, Kan.
Preston, J. W	Board of Trade	Chicago, Ills.
Pittsfield, Capt. O. A	La. Cotton Manuf	New Orleans, La.
Roache, Hon. A. L	City	Indianapolis, Ind.
Ritsinger, Fred	City	Indianapolis, Ind.
Ray, Wm. R	City	Louisville, Ky.
Rubel, W. F	City	Louisville, Ky.
Ray, Dr. Edwin S	City	Atlanta, Ga.
Ridenour, J G	City	Baltimore, Md.
Rothert, H. W	City	Keokuk, Iowa.
Remelin, Hon. Chas	City	Cincinnati, O.
Resor, Wm	City	Cincinnati, O.
Rowland, C. W	Cham. of Com	Cincinnati, O.
Reid, Saml. V	Cham. of Com	Cincinnati, O.
Raiford, Col. P. H	Board of Trade	Jacksonville, Fla.
Rathbourn, Hon. W. P	City	Chattanooga, Tenn.
Rees, David E	City	Rockwood, Tenn.
Roller, Hon. Jno. E	State	Harrisburg, Va.
Rawson, L. Q	State	Fremont, O.
Rhodes, Chas. R	State	Marietta, O.

NAMES OF DELEGATES.	REPRESENTING.	CITIES.
Reynolds, Hon. R. M	State	Montgomery, Ala.
Richardson, D	State	Galveston, Tex.
Robertson, Jno. B	State	New Orleans, La.
Sykes, Hon. W. J	Cham. of Com	Memphis, Tenn.
Snyder, H. N	Board of Trade	Chattanooga, Tenn.
Smith, Hon. H. A	Rome Iron Manuf. Co	Rome, Ga.
Smith, Henry H	Ga. & Ala. Steamboat Co.	Rome, Ga.
Senior, James N	Cornwall Iron W. Co	Rome, Ga.
Schley, Dr. Jas. M	City	Savannah, Ga.
Stetson, W. S	City	Savannah, Ga.
Styles, Col. C. W	City	Albany, Ga.
Speights, A M	State	Griffin, Ga.
Sleeper, Gen. H. S	State	Leavenworth, Kan.
Smith, Hon. Z. F	Cum. & Ohio R. R	Eminence, Ky.
Scott, Harris	Jeff. & Ind R. R	Louisville, Ky.
Spillman. James	City	Covington, Ky.
Smith, Geo. B	State	Wooster, O.
Seasongood, Lewis	City	Cincinnati, O.
Simpkinson, Jno	City	Cincinnati, O.
Shaw, Thos. F	City	Cincinnati, O.
Stewart, Capt. J. B	Tenn. River Transp. Co.	Decatur, Ala.
Sadler, O. M	Board of Trade	Charleston, S. C.
Stannard, Hon. E. O	Union Merch. Ex	St. Louis, Mo.
Sturgeon, Hon. I	State	St. Louis, Mo.
Stewart, J. R	J. R. Stewart & Co	Madison, Ind.
Storey, P. R	City	New Albany, Ind.
Stringer, Hon. T. W	City	Vicksburg, Miss.
Stafford, E	State	Jackson, Miss.
Sherer, J. W	City	New Orleans, La.
Suit, S. Taylor	State	Silverhill, Md.
Sweitzer, Gen. J. B	State	Pittsburg, Pa.
Seymour, Chas	State	La Crosse, Wis.
Shan, W. B	Boston, T. & N. Y. Com.	Washington, D. C.
Torrence, Jas. F	City	Cincinnati, O.
Taylor, S. Lester	Cham. of Com	Cincinnati, O
Thompson, S. P	Board of Trade & City	Baltimore, Md.
Throckmorton, Gov. G. W.	Transp. Cont. R. R. Co	Austin, Tex.
Turner, Jas. R	Produce Exch	New York City.
Thomas, Jno. T	State	Savannah, Ga.
Turner, G. P. M	State	Goodman, Miss.
Turner, Thomas	State	Mount Sterling, Ky.
Thompson, Hon. J	Cham. of Com	Memphis, Tenn.
Twichell, C. C	City	New Orleans, La.
Tebbetts, J. M	Mem. & Ark. Riv. Pack. Co.	Arkansas.
Underwood, P. L	Board of Trade	Chicago, Ills.
Vallandigham, Hon. C. L.	Hon. Delegate	Dayton, O.
Wilder, Jno. T	3d Cong. Dist	Chattanooga, Tenn.
Warder, Jas. A	State	Shelbyville, Tenn.
Wheeler, X	Chatt. R. Mill Co	Chattanooga, Tenn.
Wheeles, Capt. J. F	Nash. & N. W. R. R	Nashville, Tenn.

SOUTHERN COMMERCIAL CONVENTION.

NAMES OF DELEGATES.	REPRESENTING.	CITIES.
Williamson, Jas. M	Miss. & Tenn. R. R.	Memphis, Tenn.
Woodruff, W. W	City	Knoxville, Tenn.
Wickersham, M. D	City	Mobile, Ala.
Wilcox, Hon. G. H	City	Mobile, Ala.
Whitman, Ezra	City	Baltimore, Md.
Wolvington, Jas. W	City	Baltimore, Md.
Webb, Hon. Jas	State	Baltimore, Md.
Walker, W. W	State	Oldham X Roads, Va.
Wood, Col. W. W	State	Richmond, Va.
Williams, B. D	State	Little Rock, Ark.
Wolfley, Louis	State	New Orleans, La.
Williamson, J. J	City	New Orleans, La.
Woodrow, David T	City	Cincinnati, O.
Wolff, Isaac	City	Cincinnati, O.
Whetstone, T. D. S.	City	Cincinnati, O.
Watters, J. M	City	Cincinnati, O.
Wood, Wm	Eagle White Lead Co.	Cincinnati, O.
Wood, B. W	Board of Trade	Louisville, Ky.
Walling, W	Board of Trade	Louisville, Ky.
Wrightson, Hon. Thos	City	Newport, Ky.
Wilson, Jesse B	City	Washington, D. C.
Watterson, Hon. H. M	Hon. Delegate	Washington, D. C.
Wheeler, Chas. W	Board of Trade	Chicago, Ills.
Wallard, Geo. A	Board of Trade	Portsmouth, O.
Withers, C. A	City	Augusta, Ga.
Wilmot, Wm	City	Detroit, Mich.
Young, J. T	Ettrick Manuf. Co.	Petersburg, Va.
Young, J. T	City	Petersburg, Va.
Young, Col. Isaac	City	Leavenworth, Kan.

All of which is respectfully submitted.

N. P. BANKS, Chairman.

W. P. RATHBURN, Secretary.

Gen. BANKS: Mr. Chairman, I move the report be accepted, and the delegates as reported be admitted to seats in this Convention.

Carried.

The CHAIRMAN: The report of the Committee on Permanent Organization will now be in order.

Mr. S. W. MORTON, of Kentucky, Chairman of the Committee on Permanent Organization, then submitted the following report:

CINCINNATI, Oct. 4, 1870.

The Committee on Permanent Organization beg leave to make the following report:

(1st.) As *Permanent Chairman* of the Southern Commercial Convention we offer the name of Hon. JOHN W. GARRETT of Baltimore.

(2d.) For Vice Presidents of the Convention: Alabama, Col. M. D. Wickersham; Arkansas, Capt. Jno. C. Maccabe; Florida, R B. Hilton; Georgia, R. L. Mott; Iowa, T. M. Monroe; Illinois, J. W. Preston; Indiana, Hon. Willard Carpenter; Kentucky, James Bridgeford; Kansas, Maj. H. S. Sleeper; Louisiana, John H. Kennard; Mississippi, Gen. E. Stafford; Maryland, Hon. R. C. Halliday; Missouri, Gov. E. O. Stannard; Michigan, J. J. Newell; Massachusetts, Gen. N. P. Banks; New York, Col. B. P. Baker; Nevada, John G. Fox; North Carolina, J. C. Mills; Ohio, Gov. A. G. McBurney; Pennsylvania, ; South Carolina, Wm. S. Hastio; Tennessee, M. Burnes; Texas, Gov. J. W. Throckmorton; Virginia, Gen. Joseph R. Anderson; Wisconsin, Breese J. Stevens.

(3d.) *Secretaries*—H. H. Tatem, A. W. Mullen, and W. R. Bowes.

(4th.) *Reading Clerk*—Julius F. Blackburn.

At the same time making it the duty of the Chairman of the Committee on Permanent Organization upon consultation with the Secretaries to appoint such Assistant Secretaries as may be deemed necessary. Respectfully submitted,

S. W. MORTON, Chairman.

GEO. E. DODGE, Secretary.

On motion, JAMES S. GIBBONS was named as Vice President from the State of Pennsylvania.

On motion of S. W. MORTON, of Kentucky, the report of the Committee was adopted.

The Chair then appointed Gen. N. P. BANKS, of Massachusetts, and THEODORE COOK, of Ohio, to escort Hon. JOHN W. GARRETT to the Chair.

On assuming the duties of Chairman of the Southern Commercial Convention, Mr. GARRETT said:

GENTLEMEN OF THE CONVENTION:

I can not thank you in terms too strong for the very high and unexpected honor which you have conferred upon me in calling me to preside over a Convention composed of so many able and so many distinguished citizens, and upon an occasion so interesting. It is an honor which I most highly appreciate.

Rarely in our history has a similar occasion been presented. For the first time since the terrible conflict through which our country has passed, we find representatives from all the Southern States assembled upon the soil of a so-styled Northern State—the great State of Ohio—and those representatives welcomed by the eloquent and distinguished gentlemen who have just addressed you as the organs of public sentiment in such terms of warmth and hospitality and kindness, as to make all feel that the Union is truly restored and that cordiality and fraternity again exist between the North and the South. (Cheers.)

This great, splendid and hospitable city—the Queen City of the West—appreciates her relations with the South. Her geographical position is such, that with the enterprise of her citizens she can command, with the growth of the country, the grandest future. Ohio recognizes, and those Northern States, whose eminent representatives are here to-day, recognize that the early restoration of the material prosperity of the South will advance the interests of the whole people.

What can be more advantageous to the entire country than to build up the South—the South so desolated and so ruined by the recent terrible conflict? Let all be done that the South asks to restore her strength and prosperity and the happiness of her people. Let earnest influences be brought to secure National legislation that will improve her rivers and her harbors; that will construct permanent levees for the Mississippi river, and that will aid in building the great Southern Pacific Railway. (Cheers.) Do all these great things, supremely useful and invaluable to the South as they must prove in her period of calamity, and you simply do that which is comprehensive and enlightened for our national interests. (Cheers.)

To accomplish the results which should flow from the efforts of such a Convention, local interests and local feelings must—and I am sure will—be thrown aside. Harmony and co-operation will be essential to insure success; and that effective harmony and co-operation are indicated by the high character of this assemblage.

At the close of the war what was more interesting to thoughtful citizens in the North than to find the great heroes—the soldiers and leaders of the South—instead of seeking homes in foreign lands remaining in their country, standing by and with their people, and prepared, after illustrating their splendid valor in the field, to aid, when their cause was lost, in reorganizing society—in rebuilding and strengthening all the broken interests of their people, and in binding together again, in bonds of peace and fraternity, our great national Union! (Cheers.)

What magnificent examples of moral courage and grand action have been shown by many of the heroic soldiers of the South! That illustrious, great and good man, General Robert E. Lee (cheers) at the close of the war threw aside the sword and became the honored and recognized leader, in a spirit of personal independence and moral heroism, in the new work which was requisite for the South. (Cheers.) He became the president of a college, promptly throwing his energies and influence for the cause of learning, recognizing that "knowledge is power," and that the strength of the South must in the future, as always, largely depend upon the education of her sons. But, gentlemen, recent intercourse with that distinguished man has impressed me with the breadth and nobleness of his views upon other great subjects in connection with the restoration of peace and in the interests of our common country.

At a very recent period, controlled by his conviction of the importance of binding the North and the South by the strongest ties of interest and commercial relations, in addition to his labors as the president of Washington College, he accepted the presidency of a railway.

The great object of that railway—the Valley Railroad of Virginia—is to connect the Maryland system of railways through the interior with that of the Central and the extreme South, embracing the States of Virginia, Tennessee, Georgia, Alabama, Mississippi, and Louisiana. In undertaking this duty, and governed by such motives, his anxiety has been not only to labor himself, but to give an example, the value of which all must recognize, by showing that he desired to aid practically that which he believed to be the true, great and beneficent policy now and for the future to bind in cordial interest and fraternity the North and the South, the East and the West, under the flag of our common country. (Cheers.)

Direct trade, gentlemen, as stated in your programme, is to be the leading subject of discussion. Direct trade is what the South needs; and direct trade in its most enlarged sense, to embrace not only foreign commerce, but home business, to secure for each section its shortest and most economical route to the ocean, and so to organize that its regions shall become studded with manufactories; that the cotton of the South shall be made into clothing for the Southern people in the vicinity of the plantations on which it is grown, and that the surplus of its cereals and provisions shall be consumed by the employés of its factories. Let trade be so controlled as to abolish in all practical cases charges and costs and middlemen. These great interests require your most thoughtful attention and influence; and the promotion of these interests is gradually being recognized as of vital moment for our national progress. Legions of earnest patriots recognize not only the necessity for the early restoration of the material progress of the South, but that the adoption of the policy to secure a speedy restoration of all her constitutional rights, of equality and fraternity, will give the greatest prosperity and power to the Union. (Cheers.)

The South has immediate and important relations and interests in connection with the General Government. Her whole people have those interests in common. The white man and the black man of the South will be alike affected by future national legislation. The tariff that will suit the one race necessarily maintains the interests of the other.

Their interests in connection with all the great material subjects of national legislation being identical, at no distant period their co-operation and their efforts in behalf of those plain interests will, in conjunction with the aid of the North and the West, give to the South that power and prosperity which the interests of the whole country demand.

Your influence and aid, gentlemen, can bring about retrenchment and economy in the vast expenses of our Government, and thus, while honorably fulfilling every public financial obligation, legitimately, effectively and largely reduce the present severe burdens of taxation. The subjects of finance and taxation affect every citizen, and they are presented for the most serious consideration of the Convention.

I regret, gentlemen, that your choice has fallen upon one who, though most earnest to serve you—most anxious, as are his fellow citizens of the State which he has the honor to represent in this Convention, to do all which will at the earliest period restore your prosperity and effect those improvements you desire—yet is entirely inexperienced as a presiding officer of such a body.

I must therefore trust to your indulgence and your co-operation. I know the high courtesy and dignity that each member of this Convention maintains in his individual relations. May I ask that that same consideration shall be extended to the Chair in performing its duty, and for your co-operation to accomplish promptly and effectively the objects the Convention has in view?

Reiterating my thanks for the distinguished honor conferred upon me, I trust, impressed by the vast importance of the subjects before you, and the greatness of the interests that may be favorably affected by judicious action, that Heaven's benedictions may rest upon your efforts and labors. (Cheers.)

The CHAIR now called for the report of the Committee on Rules and Order of Business, whereupon Mr. BENJ. EGGLESTON, of Ohio, Chairman of the Committee, submitted the following:

To the Chairman of the Southern Commercial Convention:

The Committee on Rules of Order and Order of Business, beg leave to make the following report:

That the Rules of Order governing the House of Representatives of the United States be adopted by the Convention for the regulation of debate, subject to the following modifications:

1. All propositions presented to the Convention shall be submitted in writing and referred to appropriate committees without debate.

2. Speakers shall be limited in their remarks to thirty minutes.

The Committee also recommend the following Order of Business:

1. Direct trade between southern Atlantic cities and Europe, including the subject of Immigration.—(Adjourned from Louisville Convention.)
2. Southern Pacific Railroad.—(Adjourned from Louisville Convention.)
3. Continuous water line communication between the Mississippi river and the Atlantic seaboard.—(Adjourned from Louisville Convention.)
4. River navigation, canals, &c.—(Adjourned from Louisville Convention.)

5. Obstruction to river navigation by narrow span bridge piers.—(Adjourned from Louisville Convention.)
6. Removal of obstructions from the mouth of the Mississippi river.—(Adjourned from Louisville Convention.)
7. Construction of permanent levees on the Mississippi river.—(Adjourned from Louisville Convention.)
8. Finance and taxation.—(Adjourned from Louisville Convention.)
9. To abolish all toll charges on the navigable rivers of the United States.—(From Cincinnati Board of Trade.)
10. The enlargement of the more important lines of canal in the United States so as to render them navigable for vessels propelled by steam.—(From Cincinnati.)
11. The charges on passenger and freight traffic by rail and water lines.—(From Cincinnati Board of Trade.)
12. That all railway viaducts over navigable rivers, be made highways for railroad companies, which will pay their pro-rata toll on same; and that efforts be made to secure legislation to that effect.—(From Cincinnati Chamber Commerce.)
13. To abolish throughout the whole country all license imposed on commercial travelers.—(Cincinnati Board of Trade.)
14. Free trade in money.—(Cincinnati Chamber of Commerce.)
15. A settled policy in the public interest in regard to the disposition of the Government lands.—(City of Cincinnati.)
16. Improvement of seacoast, gulf and lake harbors.—(From Mobile Board of Trade.)
17. Wharfage on the navigable rivers.—(City of St. Louis.)
18. Ample railroad facilities from the Ohio river to the central south.—(From Chattanooga, Tenn.)
19. Direct and reciprocal trade with Brazil and other South American countries.—(From Dubuque, Iowa.)
20. Tares and short weights.—(From Cincinnati Chamber of Commerce.)
21. Removal of the national capitol.—(From St. Louis.)

The Committee recommend the adoption of the following resolutions:

1. *Resolved*, That the regular Standing Committees of the Louisville Convention be requested to report for the respectful consideration of the next Commercial Convention, upon the subject for which said committees were respectively raised, and that the chairmen of said regular committees be *ipso facto* members of said next Convention.

2. *Resolved*, That the name of this Convention be changed from "The Southern Commercial Convention," to that of "The National Commercial Convention."

> Respectfully submitted,
> B. EGGLESTON, Chairman.

Mr. EGGLESTON : The Committee recommend the adoption of these Rules of Order and Order of Business, and I therefore move that this report be adopted, with an amendment that the voting be *per capita*.

Mr. BRYSON moved as a substitute for Mr. EGGLESTON's amendment the following :

Resolved, That all votes shall be *per capita*, except when a division shall be called for, when each State shall have one vote for each senator and representative in Congress to which the State is entitled; provided, that when a State is not fully represented, no delegate therefrom shall be allowed to cast more than one vote.

Which was passed.

On motion of Mr. FORSHEY, of Texas, the third subject as reported by the Committee was amended by adding the words, ".and along the gulf coast."

The report of the Committee on Rules of Order and Order of Business, as thus amended, was then unanimously adopted.

On motion of Mr. COHEN, of South Carolina, the first resolution recommended by the Committee was unanimously adopted.

The question on the adoption of the second resolution recommended by the Committee created a lengthy discussion, which resulted in laying over the matter informally.

The Convention then adjourned until Wednesday morning October 5, at 9 o'clock.

SECOND DAY.

MORNING SESSION.

CINCINNATI, October 5th, 1870.

The Convention was called to order at 9.45 A. M. President JOHN W. GARRETT in the chair.

Rev. Mr. ELLIOTT, of the St. John's Episcopal church offered a prayer.

The Secretary proceeded to read the minutes of the previous session, when

On motion of Mr. PRATT, of Louisiana, the reading of the minutes was dispensed with.

A note of invitation from the Young Men's Christian Association was then read.

Gov. STANNARD, of Missouri, offered the following:

Resolved, That the sessions of this Convention shall be from 10 o'clock, A. M., until 1 o'clock, P. M., and from 3 o'clock, P. M., until 6 o'clock P. M., and from 8 o'clock P. M., until 10½ o'clock, P. M., unless the Convention otherwise orders.

Which was unanimously passed.

The CHAIRMAN: The regular order of business will now be proceeded with, viz: the appointment of the Committees by the respective delegations, one on behalf of each State, on the various subjects to be considered by the Convention. The Secretary will call the roll of States, and the Chairman of each delegation is requested to report the members of the Committees appointed by such delegations.

The Secretary proceeded to call the roll with the following result:

Subject No. 1.

DIRECT TRADE BETWEEN SOUTHERN ATLANTIC CITIES AND EUROPE, INCLUDING THE SUBJECT OF IMMIGRATION.

NAMES.	STATES.	NAMES.	STATES.
J. C. Maccabe	Arkansas.	J J. Newell	Michigan.
Peter Hamilton	Alabama.	N. P. Banks	Massachusetts.
R. B. Burrows	Florida.	Dr R. S. Newton	New York.
J. T. Thomas	Georgia.	John G. Fox	Nevada.
H. W. Rothert	Iowa.	J. C. Mills	North Carolina.
P. W. Dater	Illinois.	Joseph Kinsey	Ohio.
W. R. Bowes	Indiana.	J. S. Gibbons	Pennsylvania.
H. Beckarts	Kentucky	J. B. Cowen	South Carolina
Col. Isaac Young	Kansas.	Wm. H. Bryson	Tennessee.
W. M. Burwell	Louisiana.	D. Richardson	Texas.
H. M. Gaskill	Mississippi.	W. H. Walker	Virginia.
Robt. R. Kirkland	Maryland.		Wisconsin.
R. S. Elliott	Missouri.		

Subject No. 2.

SOUTHERN PACIFIC RAILROAD.

G. H. Wilcox	Alabama.	J. J. Newell	Michigan.
B. D. Williams	Arkansas.	N. P. Banks	Massachusetts.
H. L. Hart	Florida.	Peter Clark	New York.
V. A. Gaskill	Georgia,	John G. Fox	Nevada.
Thomas M. Monroe	Iowa.	A. A. Campbell	North Carolina.
J. W. Preston	Illinois.	R. M. Corwine	Ohio.
W. R. Bowes	Indiana.	W. D. Moore	Pennsylvania.
J. B. Bowman	Kentucky.	W. S. Hastie	South Carolina.
Col. Coffin	Kansas.	J. W. Clapp	Tennessee.
J. J. Williamson	Louisiana.	Gov. Throckmorton	Texas.
Harris Barksdale	Mississippi.	Isaac H. Carrington	Virginia.
Robert Fowler	Maryland.		Wisconsin.
J. H. Sturgeon	Missouri.		

Subject No. 3.

CONTINUOUS WATER LINE COMMUNICATION BETWEEN THE MISSISSIPPI RIVER, THE ATLANTIC SEABOARD, AND ALONG THE GULF COAST.

J. B. Stewart	Alabama.	Henry M. Cheever	Michigan.
Geo. E. Dodge	Arkansas	N. P. Banks	Massachusetts.
P. H. Raiford	Florida.	P Clark	New York.
Dr. E. S. Ray	Georgia.	John G. Fox	Nevada.
Thomas M. Monroe	Iowa.	J. C. Mills	North Carolina.
J McCauley	Illinois	Maj. S. V. Reed	Ohio.
S. E. Gilbert	Indiana.		Pennsylvania.
G. W. Chilton	Kentucky.	Geo. L. Holmes	South Carolina.
Gen. Sleeper	Kansas.	J. M. Williamson	Tennessee.
O. J. Noyes	Louisiana.	Col C. G. Forshey	Texas.
G. P. M. Turner	Mississippi.	R. W. Hughes	Virginia.
W. W. Dallan	Maryland.		Wisconsin.
Gen. C. B. Fisk	Missouri.		

SOUTHERN COMMERCIAL CONVENTION. 31

Subject No. 4.
RIVER NAVIGATION, CANALS, ETC.

NAMES.	STATES.	NAMES.	STATES.
J B Stewart	Alabama.	Levi Bishop	Michigan
J M Tebbetts	Arkanses.	N P Banks	Massachusetts
H L Hart	Florida.	Col B P Baker	New York
W W Fleuellen	Georgia.	John G Fox	Nevada
Thomas M Munroe	Iowa.	A A Campbell	North Carolina
Arthur Dixon	Illinois.	Benj Eggleston	Ohio
William Carpenter	Indiana.	W D Moore	Pennsylvania
S W Morton	Kentucky.	G F Laurey	South Carolina
Gen Sleeper	Kansas.	Gen J T Wilder	Tennessee
Dr John Carter	Louisiana.	C G Forshey	Texas
H M Gastrell	Mississippi.	Charles Martin	Virginia
S P Thompson	Maryland	Charles Seymour	Wisconsin
E A Stannard	Missouri	Jesse D Wilson	District of Col

Subject No. 5.
OBSTRUCTION TO RIVER NAVIGATION BY NARROW SPAN BRIDGE PIERS.

J M Humphrey	Alabama	Levi Bishop	Michigan
B D Williams	Arkansas	N P Banks	Massachusetts
P H Raiford	Florida	O R Baker	New York
James Noble Sen'r	Georgia	John G Fox	Nevada
Thomas N Monroe	Iowa	A A Campbell	North Carolina
Arthur Dixon	Illinois	Judge C R Rhodes	Ohio
N Powell	Indiana	Gen J B Sweitzer	Pennsylvania
A S Berry	Kentucky	Geo L Holmes	South Carolina
Judge Pendery	Kansas	John Cubbins	Tennessee
Capt O A Pittsfield	Louisiana	Gen Geo P Buell	Texas
T W Stringer	Mississippi	Chas Martin	Virginia
S P Thompson	Maryland		Wisconsin
Capt Barton Able	Missouri		

Subject No. 6.
REMOVAL OF OBSTRUCTIONS FROM MOUTH OF THE MISSISSIPPI RIVER.

J M Humphrey	Alabama	Wm Wilmot	Michigan
J C Maccabe	Arkansas	N P Banks	Massachusetts
Dr R B Burroughs	Florida	Dr R S Newton	New York
Dr J M Schley	Georgia	John G Fox	Nevada
Thomas M Monroe	Iowa	A A Campbell	North Carolina
C W Wheeler	Illinois	Judge Rhodes	Ohio
A L Roache	Indiana	J S Gibbons	Pennsylvania
J B Davis	Kentucky	Bernard O'Niel	South Carolina
Gen Sleeper	Kansas	M B Adams	Tennessee
L J Higby	Louisiana	Col C G Forshey	Texas
E Stafford	Mississippi	D T Young	Virginia
James Webb	Maryland	Charles Seymour	Wisconsin
Gen C B Fisk	Missouri		

Subject No. 7.

CONSTRUCTION OF PERMANENT LEVEES ON THE MISSISSIPPI RIVER.

NAMES.	STATES.	NAMES.	STATES.
G H Wilcox	Alabama	William Wilmot	Michigan
J C Maccabe	Arkansas	N P Banks	Massachusetts
P H Raiford	Florida	C B Camp	New York
Dr J M Schley	Georgia	John G Fox	Nevada
Thomas M Monroe	Iowa	A A Campbell	North Carolina
O S Hough	Illinois	Geo L Johnston	Ohio
H W Cloud	Indiana	J S Gibbons	Pennsylvania
Geo Ainsley	Kentucky	Bernard O'Niel	South Carolina
Gen Sleeper	Kansas	Jacob Thompson	Tennessee
J H Kennard	Louisiana	D Richardson	Texas
G P M Inmer	Mississippi	John E Roller	Virginia
Robt Garrett	Maryland		Wisconsin
M A Bryson	Missouri		

Subject No. 8.

FINANCE AND TAXATION.

M B Jonas	Alabama	Richard Hawley	Michigan
J M Tibbetts	Arkansas	N P Banks	Massachusetts
R B Burroughs	Florida	C B Camp	New York
C J Withers	Georgia	J G Fox	Nevada
H W Rother	Iowa	J C Mills	North Carolina
P L Underwood	Illinois	J C Butler	Ohio
Dr W S Pierce	Indiana	W D Moore	Pennsylvania
C R Long	Kentucky	J B Cohen	South Carolina
Col Young	Kansas	John M Bass	Tennessee
C C Buddeke	Louisiana	Gov Throckmorton	Texas
E E Overall	Mississippi	Thos Branch	Virginia
Harry Fisher	Maryland		Wisconsin
D T Jewett	Missouri	J B Wilson	Washington

Subject No. 9.

TO ABOLISH ALL TOLL CHARGES ON THE NAVIGABLE RIVERS OF THE UNITED STATES.

J B Stewart	Alabama	Richard Hawley	Michigan
B D Williams	Arkansas	N P Banks	Massachusetts
H L Hart	Florida	J R Turner	New York
A G Pitner	Georgia	John G Fox	Nevada
Thomas M Monroe	Iowa	A A Campbell	North Carolina
J W Preston	Illinois	William Resor	Ohio
F P Carson	Indiana	Capt C A Dravo	Pennsylvania
William Ernst	Kentucky	H E Lowry	South Carolina
Gen Sleeper	Kansas	C P Breed	Tennessee
T P Hotchkiss	Louisiana		Texas
Y P Prior	Mississippi	R D Lilley	Virginia
J B Brinkley	Maryland		Wisconsin
Barton Able	Missouri		

Subject No. 10.

THE ENLARGEMENT OF THE MORE IMPORTANT LINES OF CANAL IN THE UNITED STATES, ETC.

NAMES.	STATES.	NAMES.	STATES.
J M Humphrey	Alabama	S M Cutcheon	Michigan
J M Tebbetts	Arkansas	N P Banks	Massachusetts
P H Raiford	Florida	J R Turner	New York
W T Newman	Georgia	John G Fox	Nevada
Thomas M Monroe	Iowa	A A Campbell	North Carolina
James M McCauley	Illinois	G Volney Dorsey	Ohio
Dr W S Pierce	Indiana	Gen J D Sweitzer	Pennsylvania
J L Allen	Kentucky	J Barrett Cohen	South Carolina
Col Coffin	Kansas	N E Alloway	Tennessee
E T Fellows	Louisiana	Gen Buell	Texas
Harris Barkesdale	Mississippi	W M Archer	Virginia
Robt Fowler	Maryland		Wisconsin
D T Jewett	Missouri		

Subject No. 11.

CHARGES ON PASSENGER AND FREIGHT TRAFFIC.

M. B. Jonas	Alabama.	Levi Bishop	Michigan.
J. C. Maccabe	Arkansas.	N. P. Banks	Massachusetts.
R. B. Hilton	Florida.	Col. Ben. P. Baker	New York.
Dr. J. J Harris	Georgia.	John G. Fox	Nevada.
Thomas N. Monroe	Iowa.	J. C. Mills	North Carolina.
O. S. Hough	Illinois.	G. P. Smith	Ohio.
F. P. Carson	Indiana.	C. N. Dravo	Pennsylvania.
James Crutcher	Kentucky.	Wm. S. Hasty	South Carolina.
Col. Coffin	Kansas.	E. W. Cole	Tennessee.
J. H. Kennard	Louisiana.	Gov. Throckmorton	Texas.
R. S. Buck	Mississippi.	J. C. Armistead	Virginia.
T. J. McKaig, Jr	Maryland.		Wisconsin.
Richard Edwards	Missouri.		

Subject No. 12.

RAILWAY VIADUCTS OVER NAVIGABLE RIVERS, ETC.

C. A. Miller	Alabama.	Henry M. Cheever	Michigan.
B. D. Williams	Arkansas.	N. P. Banks	Massachusetts.
P. H Raiford	Florida.	O. R. Baker	New York.
W. W. Lewellen	Georgia.	John G. Fox	Nevada.
H. W. Rosket	Iowa.	A. A. Campbell	North Carolina.
I. McCauley	Illinois.	Robt. Mitchell	Ohio.
Dr. Pierce	Indiana.	W. D. Moore	Pennsylvania.
P. T. German	Kentucky.	O. M. Sadler	South Carolina.
Judge J. L. Pendray	Kansas.	W. W. Woodruff	Tennessee.
S. C. Emley	Louisiana.	Gen. Buell	Texas.
E. Stafford	Mississippi.	Joseph R. Anderson	Virginia.
H. Irvin Keyser	Maryland.		Wisconsin.
E. O. Stannard	Missouri.		

Subject No. 13.

TO ABOLISH LICENSE ON COMMERCIAL TRAVELERS.

NAMES.	STATES.	NAMES.	STATES.
L. H. Mayer	Alabama.	Wm. Wilmot	Michigan.
J. C. Maccabe	Arkansas.	N. P. Banks	Massachusetts.
R. B. Burroughs	Florida.	Col. B. P. Baker	New York.
	Georgia.	John G Fox	Nevada.
H. W. Rothert	Iowa.	A. A. Campbell	North Carolina.
P. W. Dater	Illinois.	D. B. Pierson	Ohio.
S. E. Gilbert	Indiana.	Capt. C. A. Dravo	Pennsylvania.
J. A. Krack	Kentucky.	Wm. S. Hastie	South Carolina.
Judge J. D. Pendery	Kansas.	Xen. Wheeler	Tennessee.
W. J. Behan	Louisiana.		Texas.
T. W. Stringer	Mississippi.	G. P. Prescott	Virginia.
Ezra Whitman	Maryland.		Wisconsin.
A. O. Blackman	Missouri.		

Subject No. 14.

FREE TRADE IN MONEY.

R M Reynolds	Alabama	William A Butler	Michigan
Geo E Dodge	Arkansas	N P Banks	Massachusetts
H L Hart	Florida	C D Camp	New York
Col C A Withers	Georgia	John G Fox	Nevada
H H Rothert	Iowa	J C Mills	North Carolina
O S Hough	Illinois	Charles Remelin	Ohio
H W Cloud	Indiana	Jos S Gibbons	Pennsylvania
Thomas Turner	Kentucky	1 Barrett Cohen	South Carolina
Gol W G Coffin	Kansas	William J Sykes	Tennessee
E C Hancock	Louisiana		Texas
H M Gastrell	Mississippi	R C Osborn	Virginia
R S Fowler	Maryland		Wisconsin
I H Stringer	Missouri	J B Wilson	Washingt'n C'y

Subject No. 15.

A SETTLED POLICY REGARDING PUBLIC LANDS.

C A Miller	Alabama	S M Cutcheon	Michigan
J M Tebbetts	Arkansas	N P Banks	Massachusetts
R B Hilton	Florida	J H Drake	New York
L S Baum	Georgia	John G Fox	Nevada
H M Rothert	Iowa	A A Campbell	North Carolina
A Dixon	Illinois	R M Bishop	Ohio
A L Roache	Indiana	Gen J B Switzer	Pennsylvania
S W Morton	Kentucky	W H Jones	South Carolina
Col Coffin	Kansas	Thomas M Jones	Tennessee
D C Labatt	Louisiana		Texas
C A Foster	Mississippi	B J Barbour	Virginia
Isaac George	Maryland		Wisconsin
T C Fletcher	Missouri		

SOUTHERN COMMERCIAL CONVENTION.   35

Subject No. 16.
IMPROVEMENT OF SEA COAST, LAKE AND GULF HARBORS.

NAMES.	STATES.	NAMES.	STATES.
William Miller	Alabama	Henry M Cheever	Michigan
J M Tebbetts	Arkansas	Gen N P Banks	Massachusetts
P H Raiford	Florida	P Clarke	New York
H B Capers	Georgia	John G Fox	Nevada
Thos M Monroe	Iowa	J C Mills	North Carolina
P L Underwood	Illinois	Miles Greenwood	Ohio
W R Bowes	Indiana	Capt C A Dravo	Pennsylvania
G W Chilton	Kentucky	William S Hastie	South Carolina
Col Young	Kansas	M H Clarke	Tennessee
M A Baker	Louisiana	Col C G Forshey	Texas
Col J P Prior	Mississippi	C W Button	Virginia
James Webb	Maryland		Wisconsin
A O Blackman	Missouri		

Subject No. 17.
WHARFAGE ON NAVIGABLE RIVERS.

J Y Cantwell	Alabama	Levi Bishop	Michigan
Geo E Dodge	Arkansas	N P Banks	Massachusetts
H L Hart	Florida	Dr R S Newton	New York
N S Finney	Georgia	John G Fox	Nevada
H W Rothert	Iowa	A A Campbell	North Carolina
C W Wheeler	Illinois	John D Minor	Ohio
F P Carson	Indiana	Capt C A Dravo	Pennsylvania
	Kentucky	Geo L Holmes	South Carolina
Col Young	Kansas	F P Gracey	Tennessee
J W Sheerer	Louisiana		Texas
F W Stringer	Mississippi		Virginia
J B Brinkley	Maryland		Wisconsin
M A Bryson	Missouri		

Subject No. 18.
AMPLE RAILROAD FACILITIES FROM THE OHIO RIVER TO THE CENTRAL SOUTH.

M D Wickersham	Alabama	J J Newell	Michigan
J M Tibbetts	Arkansas	N P Banks	Massachusetts
R B Hilton	Florida	O R Baker	New York
Daniel Pittman	Georgia	John G Fox	Nevada
H W Rothert	Iowa	J C Mills	North Carolina
J McCauley	Illinois	Matthew Addy	Ohio
Elijah Newland	Indiana	James L Gibbons	Pennsylvania
Julius Dorn	Kentucky	Bernard O'Neil	South Carolina
Col Coffin	Kansas	E A James	Tennessee
Louis Wolfley	Louisiana	General Buell	Texas
C A Foster	Mississippi	F T Glasgow	Virginia
John G Ridenour	Maryland		Wisconsin
R Elliott	Missouri		

Subject No. 19.

DIRECT AND RECIPROCAL TRADE WITH BRAZIL AND OTHER SOUTH AMERICAN COUNTRIES.

NAMES.	STATES.	NAMES.	STATES.
P G Clarke	Alabama	Richard Hanley	Michigan
Geo E Dodge	Arkansas	N P Banks	Massachusetts
R B Burroughs	Florida	Peter Clark	New York
C S Finney	Georgia	John G Fox	Nevada
H W Rothert	Iowa	J C Mills	North Carolina
J W Preston	Illinois	Gov A G McBirney	Ohio
P R Story	Indiana		Pennsylvania
G W Morton	Kentucky	O M Sadler	South Carolina
Col Coffin	Kansas	W P Rathburn	Tennessee
Wm M Burwell	Louisiana	D Richardson	Texas
E E Overall	Mississippi		Virginia
Robt R Kirkland	Maryland		Wisconsin
T C Fletcher	Missouri		

Subject No. 20.

TARES AND SHORT WEIGHT.

NAMES.	STATES.	NAMES.	STATES.
William Miller	Alabama	William A Butler	Michigan
J C Maccabe	Arkansas	N P Banks	Massachusetts
R B Burroughs	Florida	Col R P Baker	New York
Henry A Smith	Georgia	John G Fox	Nevada
H W Rothert	Iowa	A A Campbell	North Carolina
P W Dater	Illinois	Thomas R Biggs	Ohio
S E Gilbert	Indiana		Pennsylvania
J H Littlerlee	Kentucky	H T Laurey	South Carolina
Col Coffin	Kansas	H A Snyder	Tennessee
S C Emley	Louisiana		Texas
J P Pryor	Mississippi		Virginia
J W Wolvington	Maryland		Wisconsin
R S Elliott	Missouri	J B Wilson	Washington C'y

Subject No. 21.

REMOVAL NATIONAL CAPITAL.

NAMES.	STATES.	NAMES.	STATES.
Geo E Dodge	Arkansas	Wm A Butler	Michigan
J M Humphrey	Alabama	N P Banks	Massachusetts
R B Hilton	Florida	J H Drake	New York
H D Capers	Georgia	John G Fox	Nevada
H W Rothert	Iowa	J C Miller	North Carolina
A Dixon	Illinois	N C McLean	Ohio
S E Gilbert	Indiana		Pennsylvania
	Kentucky	Wm S Hastie	South Carolina
Judge J L Pendery	Kansas	J A Warder	Tennessee
Dr John Carter	Louisiana	Col C G Forshey	Texas
C A Foster	Mississippi	J C Hill	Virginia
R C Halliday	Maryland		Wisconsin
Barton Able	Missouri	J D Wilson	Washington C'y

It was ordered that the name of Captain E. E. OVERALL, of Mississippi, be placed upon the roll of the Convention to fill a vacancy in the delegation from that State.

The same action was taken on Captain O. A. PITTSFIELD, of Louisiana.

Mr. WICKERSHAM, of Alabama, offered the following:

WHEREAS, That we regard it of national importance to secure unobstructed navigation in the Tennessee river, from its mouth to Decatur, Alabama; therefore,

Resolved, That we earnestly consider that the Congress of the United States could in no manner more wisely apply any part of the public money than by an ample appropriation to widen the canal throughout the Mussel shoals of that river.

Which was referred to the Committee on River Navigation, Canals, &c.

On motion of Gov. STANNARD, of Missouri, the reports of the various Committees of the Louisville Convention, were ordered to be referred to the proper Committees of the Convention for consideration, without being read.

Mr. WICKERSHAM, of Alabama, by general consent, offered the following:

Resolved, That no delegate or delegates from any particular State shall be permitted to occupy more than thirty minutes, until every other State represented on the floor of the Convention shall have an equal amount of time, if said State desires to consume it.

After a lengthy discussion, Mr. CORWINE, of Ohio, offered the following substitute:

Resolved, That no member of this Convention be allowed to speak more than ten minutes on any subject, unless otherwise ordered by this Convention.

Which was adopted.

Gov. STANNARD, of Missouri, offered the following:

Resolved, That the Representatives of the valley of the Mississippi in Congress, be requested to introduce bills for the increase and equalization of postal steam service, by additional subsidies to lines of steamers between the port of New Orleans and the principal ports of Europe, America and Asia.

Which was referred to the Committee on Direct Trade between Southern Atlantic Cities and Europe.

Also the following:

WHEREAS, There exist State charters for a railroad from St. Louis to Mount Carmel, in the State of Illinois, and from Mount Carmel to Louisville, Kentucky, and from Louisville to Pound Gap, and from Pound Gap to Wythville, West Virginia, and from Wythville to Norfolk, Virginia, making a continuous air-line from Norfolk, Virginia, to St. Louis, Missouri: therefore, be it

Resolved, That this Convention recommend to the United States Congress the granting of a National Railroad Charter over the routes above named, from Norfolk, Virginia, to St. Louis, Missouri, to be known as the Air-Line Railroad, from Norfolk *via* Louisville to St. Louis.

Which was referred to the Committee on Ample Railroad facilities between the Ohio River and the Central South.

On motion of Mr. BARBOUR, of Virginia, a special committee of five was ordered appointed, by the Chair, on the subject of railroads to connect the cities of Virginia with the great west.

Mr. CLARK, of New York, offered the following:

WHEREAS, The geographical position of the United States, their vast territory and extent of sea-coast, their noble rivers, lakes, gulfs and bays, the variety and importance of their agricultural productions and boundless deposits of mineral wealth, give assurance that under the energizing influence of free institutions they are destined soon to become the first maritime power of the earth; and

WHEREAS, The opening of the Suez Canal, diverting the commerce of the world into new channels, and giving it flow through the Mediterranean across the Atlantic to our own ports, and over our continental railways of the Pacific, presents a golden opportunity to our country to revive her shipping interest and regain her commercial pre-eminence; therefore,

Resolved, That in the opinion of this Convention, Congress should take prompt and efficient action to aid in the construction of iron steamships in American shipyards, instead of a humiliating dependence on foreign nations, and to place in the hands of our own citizens the control of our international trade.

Resolved, That the Mediterranean Oriental Steam Navigation Company, of New York, as the pioneer in this great enterprise designed to connect by a steamship line New York, Norfolk and other Southern ports, with Cadiz, Marseilles, Genos, Trieste and other Mediterranean ports, and to introduce from Southern Europe into the Southern States an intelligent population accustomed to the culture of their great staples, merits the approbation of this Convention, and is warmly recommended to the liberal patronage of the General Government.

Which was referred to the Committee on Direct Trade between Southern Atlantic Cities and Europe.

Mr. EGGLESTON, of Ohio, offered the following:

Resolved, That the District of Columbia be added to the list of States to be called when the roll of States is called, in the regular order of business.

Which was adopted.

On motion of Mr. ALLOWAY, of Tennessee, it was

Resolved, That no resolution shall be acknowledged by the chair, nor discussed by this Convention, until the same is reduced to writing and read by the Secretary, motions to adjourn and calls for the previous question only excepted.

Mr. STURGEON, of Missouri, offered the following:

WHEREAS, The Omaha Pacific Railway was built largely out of the aid furnished by the National Government, on a line that we believe would not have been adopted had all the States been represented in Congress; and

WHEREAS, Its location unjustly taxes the business interests of a large section of the country south of Omaha, by subjecting it to long transit charges before it reaches Omaha, the starting point for the Pacific Coast; and

WHEREAS, It is the duty of the Government to confer, as far as possible, equal benefits on all sections of the country when using the public funds to promote a public interest; and

WHEREAS, The Omaha Pacific Railroad can never be made to

subserve equitably the interests of the whole country by reasons of its location so far North; and

WHEREAS, Another Pacific Railroad is imperatively demanded to produce a healthful competition, whereby the rates for freight and travel may be reduced, and greater accommodations for the public; and

WHEREAS, Justice to the whole country demands that the United States Government shall grant such liberal subsidies, and all such other needed legislation, as will secure the most speedy construction of another great National Pacific road, on a more central National route, which will more equitably subserve the interests of the whole country; therefore,

Resolved, That this Convention memorialize Congress to grant such liberal subsidies, and all such other needed legislation, as will secure the earliest possible construction of a more National Central Pacific Railroad to San Francisco and San Diego.

Resolved, That Congress be memorialized to grant such aid as will secure the construction of railroads to connect the railway system of the country, north and south, with the great central line, to the end that all sections of the Union may have, as near as possible, equal advantages from short connections with the great National Pacific Railroads of the country.

Resolved, That the delegations of each State be requested to ask of the Legislatures of their respective States, and also of cities to appoint agents who shall attend the sittings of Congress, and render such aid as they may have it in their power to their respective Congressional delegations in preparing statistics, and all information that will tend to secure the legislation required for the accomplishment of the great objects embraced in the foregoing preamble and resolutions.

Resolved, That a committee of one from each State represented in this Convention be raised to prepare and present to Congress a memorial setting forth more at large the reasons which exist for the speediest possible construction of another great national railway on a line that will equitably subserve the interests of the country, not yet provided with the advantages that flow from close proximity to the Eastern terminus of a completed National Pacific Railroad.

Which was referred to Committee on Southern Pacific Railroad.

Mr. COLE, of Tennessee, offered the following:

Resolved, That all breaks and obstructions in our great highways of trade and travel be remedied, and the connection of tracks and uniformity of gauge be perfected as early as possible, so that trains may pass from one road to another without annoyance or delay, whether passengers or freight.

Which on motion of the same gentleman was referred to a special committee of one from each State on Railroads Generally, to be appointed by the chair.

A delegate from Kentucky offered the following :

WHEREAS, The Cumberland and Ohio Railroad Company, with chartered privileges from the Legislatures of Kentucky and Tennessee, having obtained subscriptions of stock to the amount of nearly four million dollars in the States named for the purpose of completing direct railroad communications between the Ohio River and Nashville, McMinnville and Chattanooga, and at those points with the entire railway system of the South, thus connecting the railway systems of the Northern States with those of the Southern, and traversing sections of the two States named of great natural wealth and advantages, but destitute of railroad facilities; and

WHEREAS, The advanced condition of this enterprise renders it a feasible and practicable plan for the early construction of this most important line of railway communication, and at comparatively small additional aid from interests, corporations, or large commercial cities ; therefore,

Resolved, That the proposed lines of railway are not only of great value to the sections traversed, but essential to the prosperity and development of the commerce, trade and wealth of the Mississippi Valley, and of national importance.

Resolved, That this Convention indorse this enterprise as one of inestimable value to the country, and recommend its claims to the common favor of the interested public for its approval, and for material aid to hasten its consummation to success.

Which was referred to the Committee on Ample Railroad Facilities between the Ohio River and the Central South.

Mr. ABLE of Missouri, offered the following :

Resolved, That in view of the rapid increase of population in the valley of the Mississippi, and the widely extended increase of our population in the Far West, it is deemed expedient and proper by this Convention to urge upon the people of this country the early removal of the National Capital to the valley of the Mississippi.

Referred to the Committee on Removal of the National Capital.

Mr. CAPERS, of Georgia, presented letters referring to the Eastern terminus of the Southern Pacific Railroad, on Railroads generally, and on Finance, which were referred to the appropriate Committees without reading.

Mr. BURWELL, of Louisiana, presented a resolution which was referred to the Committee on Removal of Obstructions from the mouth of the Mississippi River.

(This resolution not having been reported back by the Committee, can not be given here.)
SECRETARY.

Mr. FORSHEY, of Texas, offered the following :

Resolved, That a special committee be raised to consider the translatitudinal railroads in the United States; the committee to consist of five members appointed by the Chair, with the privilege of any State delegation to add a member to that committee.

Which was adopted.

Mr. WILMOT, of Michigan, offered the following :

Resolved, That the Committee on Finance and Taxation be, and they are hereby requested to report to the Convention as to the feasibility of abolishing all National banks and substituting in lieu thereof the issue of a legal-tender currency by the National Government.

Referred to Committee on Finance and Taxation.

Mr. HOTCHKISS, of Louisiana, offered the following :

Resolved, That in the opinion of this Convention the importance of the agricultural productions of the Red River of Louisiana deserves at the hands of Congress an appropriation for the removal of the raft and other obstructions in said river.

Referred to Committee on River Navigation.

Mr. SUIT, of Maryland, offered the following :

WHEREAS, Mr. J. B. Wilson, being the only delegate present from the District of Columbia; therefore, be it

Resolved, That he be placed on all the Standing Committees of this Convention, as representative from the District of Columbia.

Adopted.

Mr. CAPERS, of Georgia, offered the following:

Resolved, That the present condition of the Southern harbors on the Atlantic and Gulf coasts, and the constantly increasing business of these several sea ports, requires that the General Government should grant liberal appropriations for the removal of obstructions existing in said harbors, and for dredging the same.

Resolved, That whereas the port of Savannah has been unsuccessful heretofore in obtaining an appropriation for the aforesaid purpose, and that said city is the only one in which obstructions exist which has not been granted an appropriation, that the improvement of the harbor of the city of Savannah be specially brought to the attention of Congress, and that this Convention recommend a liberal appropriation for this end.

Referred to the Committee on Sea coast Harbors.

Mr. KINSEY, of Ohio, offered the following:

WHEREAS, We meet in Convention to compare views that will indicate the public vision of National affairs, desiring nothing but the general welfare of our great National Union of States; therefore,

Resolved, That we declare for the full and final payment of our public debt, the revenue to be collected from a tax on spirits, malt liquors and tobacco, and a tariff discriminating in favor of our own workmen and capitalists, that will develop the resources of our common country, increase the number of our manufactures, give steady employment to more laborers, cause the immigration of skilled labor, the lessening of prices to consumers, the creating of a permanent home market for agricultural products, overcome the necessity for the odious and expensive internal taxation, and which will soon enable us to compete with the manufacturers of Europe in the markets of the world.

Which was referred to Committee on Finance and Taxation.

Mr. BUTLER, of Michigan, offered the following:

Resolved, That we are in favor of a tariff for purposes of revenue only; that duties should never be levied with a view to give one branch of industry, or one section of the country, an advantage over others; that the rates should be fixed with regard solely to revenue, and should be made to bear as equally and as lightly as possible on all branches of industry, and upon all sections of the country.

Which was referred to Committee on Finance and Taxation.

A delegate offered the following:

WHEREAS, The Ohio River forms a link in the grand chain of communication between the Western States and the Gulf of Mexico on the one hand, and on the other with the Atlantic seaboard; therefore,

Resolved, That this Convention respectfully and earnestly recommend that the Congress of the United States make an appropriation for the improvement of the Ohio River.

Which was referred to Committee on River Navigation, Canals, etc.

Mr. CHILTON, of Kentucky, offered the following

PREAMBLE: Regarding the question of the removal of the National Capital as one of a political character, and not coming within the legitimate scope of the business and purposes of this Convention, it is

Resolved, That it will not be considered by this body, and that its announcement as a subdivision on the Order of Business be stricken therefrom.

Resolved, That the Committee on the Removal of the National Capital be at once discharged.

Which was referred to Committee on Rules and Order of Business.

Mr. TURNER, of Mississippi, offered the following:

Resolved, That in the opinion of this Convention the State of Mississippi should control and manage her own levee system, and to secure which appropriate legislation is recommended to the Congress of the United States.

Which was referred to Committee on Mississippi River Levees.

Mr. ELLIOTT, of Missouri, offered the following:

WHEREAS, A continuous line of railway now connects the cities of the Mississippi valley with Denver, at the base of the Rocky mountains, in Colorado, through the State of Kansas; and

WHEREAS, It is desirable for all interests in the central belt of States that said railway be extended to the Pacific coast by the most direct line possible: therefore,

Resolved, That Congress be memorialized to extend aid, in lands and subsidies, to a line of railway passing south of the line now occupied by the Union Pacific Railway, and reaching from the present line in Kansas to the Pacific ocean at San Diego and San Francisco.

Which was referred to Committee on Southern Pacific Railroad.

The following, offered by Prof. R. C. HALLIDAY, of Maryland, was referred to the Committee on Rules and Order of Business:

PREAMBLE: Recognizing the importance of the diffusion of knowledge among all classes of society, and the people at large, by a proper system of education, and deeming it worthy the consideration of a commercial convention,

Resolved, That a committee, to be called the Committee on Education, be appointed by the Chair, who shall give the subject due and proper consideration, and report on the same at the next session of the Commercial Convention.

Mr. DRAKE, of New York, offered the following.

WHEREAS, The Erie canal of the State of New York is a great highway of commerce, and the question of cheap transportation being one of vital interest to the producing section of the great West; therefore, be it

Resolved, That we recommend Congress to make sufficient appropriation for the purchase of the Erie canal of New York, and the abolishment of tolls now existent with said canal.

Referred to Committee on River Navigation, Canals, &c.

Mr. PRYOR, of Mississippi, offered the following:

Resolved, That the construction of a short-line railroad, eighteen miles long, from Corinth, Mississippi, to Hamburg, Tennessee, on the Tennessee river, is a project in which all the cities on the upper Ohio and Mississippi are interested, and has the cordial indorsement of this Convention.

Referred to the Committee on Railroads Generally.

A communication was presented from Gen. DUFF GREEN, of Kentucky, in relation to the Government authorizing subscriprions in aid of the construction of railroads, which was referred without reading to the Committee on Railroads Generally.

Mr. BEHAN, of Louisiana, offered the following:

WHEREAS, Congress has recently abolished all special licenses and taxes on all trades and professions except that of wholesale liquor and Tobacco dealers, and it being the opinion of the commercial community at large that the continuance of this license and tax on those dealing in the above articles bears unjustly and inconveniently on those merchants who are compelled to trade in liquors and tobaccos. We would therefore suggest and recommend to the next Congress the following resolation:

Resolved, That this Convention would recommend the abolishment of all special licenses and taxes on wholesale liquor and tobacco dealers.

Be it further resolved, If those sources of revenue are necessary to the Government, it is recommended that the taxes be increased at the place of manufacture.

Which was referred to the Committee on Finance and Taxation.

Mr. HANCOCK, of Louisiana, offered the following:

WHEREAS, The traveling public of this country is now, through lack of legislation, left entirely at the mercy of the railroad corporations to which its safety and interests are intrusted; and

WHEREAS, It is one of the main provinces of the government to protect the interest of the public in all contracts made with individuals or private corporations; therefore, be it

Resolved, That in the opinion of this Convention some Congressional or State legislation is imperatively due to the traveling public, in order to secure the faithful fulfillment of all contracts made and implied by the sale and purchase of transportation tickets, so as to effectually guard it against further imposition in the way of deficient and extortionate refectories, and to better secure it in proper provisions for safety, despatch and comfort.

Referred to Committee on Railroads Generally.

Mr. MACCABE, of Arkansas, offered the following:

WHEREAS, The commercial relations of the United States with Europe being variously disturbed by the present calamitous war between France and Prussia; and

WHEREAS, The best interests of Europe and America are to be consulted in the establishment of permanent peace between the belligerents; therefore,

Resolved, That this Convention, representing the commercial interests of the whole country, earnestly invokes the friendly interposition of the United States government, looking to the establishment of a speedy peace between the republic of France and the kingdom of Prussia.

Which, under a suspension of the rules, was, on motion of the same gentleman, referred to a special committee of five, to be appointed by the Chair.

Mr. WILDER, of Tennessee, offered the following:

Resolved, That in any recommendation to Congress, asking for subsidy to aid in the construction of a Southern Pacific Railway, provision be made for three termini on the Mississippi River, viz.: one opposite New Orleans, one opposite Vicksburg, and one opposite Memphis; and that all of said branches be entitled to equal and reciprocal advantages in the transmission of freights and passengers and rates of charges with the main line; and that the main line shall pro rate with them, and a subsidy of lands be granted in aid of the branches as well as the main line.

Which was referred to the Committee on Southern Pacific Railroad.

Mr. CAMPBELL, of North Carolina, offered the following, which was referred to the Committee on Railroads Generally:

WHEREAS, The State of North Carolina ceded to the United States the territory (now State) of Tennessee, an area of land surpassing in excellence and richness that derived from any other source except the North-west territory ceded by Virginia; and

WHEREAS, One of the great highways from the Southern Pacific Railroad to the middle East lies through her mountain lands; therefore,

Resolved, That we recommend the passage by the United States Congress of a liberal appropriation to the Transatlantic road and the Western N. C. Railroad.

Mr. BOWMAN offered the following :

WHEREAS, The Southern Commercial Convention, now in session, by its liberal policy and comprehensive action, has invited and secured a representation of the various commercial and industrial interests of the whole country, and has thereby assumed a national character and importance, therefore be it

Resolved, That when this Convention adjourns it will meet at ——————, on ————————, 1871, under the name and style of the National Commercial Convention.

Which, on motion of the same gentleman, was made the special order for 11 o'clock, A. M., Friday, Oct. 7.

Mr. SEYMOR, of Wisconsin, offered a resolution relative to the disposition of the public lands of that State, which was referred without reading to the Committee on a Settled Policy in relation to the Disposition of Public Lands.

On motion of Mr. CAPERS, of Georgia, the Convention adjourned until 9 o'clock, A. M., of Thursday, Oct. 6.

THIRD DAY.

MORNING SESSION.

The Convention was called to order at 10 A. M., President GARRETT in the Chair.

Prayer was offered by Rev. WM. T. MOORE.

On motion, the reading of the minutes of the preceding day was dispensed with.

Mr. COOK, of Ohio, by the unanimous consent of the Convention, offered the following:

Resolved, That the Cincinnati Commercial Convention cordially indorses the paper signed by the officers of the Memphis, New Orleans, Louisville and Cincinnati Commercial Convention, recommending the endowment of a Department of Commerce in Washington College, Virginia.

Which was adopted.

The Chair announced the following special committees, ordered appointed by previous action of the Convention:

ON FRANCO-PRUSSIAN WAR.—J. C. Maccabe, Arkansas; Gen. N. P. Banks, Massachusetts; Gen. Jos. R. Anderson, Virginia; Theo. Cook, Ohio; John H. Kennard, Louisiana.

ON TRANS-LATITUDINAL ROADS IN THE UNITED STATES.—C. G. Forshey, Texas; R. S. Elliott, Missouri; R. M. Bishop, Ohio; J. C. Burch, Pennsylvania; Charles R. Long, Kentucky.

IN REFERENCE TO RAILROADS TO CONNECT THE CITIES OF VIRGINIA WITH THE GREAT WEST.—B. F. Barbour, Virginia; Geo. F. Davis, Ohio; James Bridgeford, Kentucky; Willard Carpenter, Indiana; M. Burns, Tennessee.

ON RAILWAYS GENERALLY.—E. W. Cole, Tennessee; M. D. Wickersham, Alabama; R. P. Hilton, Florida; James M. Schley, Georgia; P. W. Baker, Illinois; B. D. Williams, Arkansas; T. M. Monroe, Iowa; John W. Grubbs, Indiana; Col. J. W. Coffin, Kansas; Wm. Ernst, Kentucky; D. C. Labott, Louisiana; Isaac H. Sturgeon, Missouri; James J. Newell, Michigan; Gen. E. Stafford, Mississippi; N. P. Banks, Massachusetts; B. P. Baker, New York; Theodore Cook, Ohio; James S. Gibbons, Pennsylvania; J. Barrett Cohen, South Carolina; G. A. Throckmorton, Texas; John E. Rollen, Virginia; D. M. Kelley, Wisconsin; Jesse B. Wilson, District of Columbia; Samuel P. Thompson, Maryland.

Mr. SNYDER, of Tennessee: Mr. Chairman, I move that a committee of one from each State be appointed by the Chair to select and report a place for the next meeting of the Convention, and to fix the basis of representation thereto.

Carried.

Mr. EMLY, of Louisiana, offered the following:

Resolved, That the Committee on "Obstructions to Navigation by Narrow Span Bridge Piers," are hereby requested to consider also hight of bridges crossing navigable waters.

Which was referred to Committee on Obstruction to River Navigation by Narrow Span Bridges.

The Chair then announced that the reports of the regular Standing Committees of the Convention would be in order.

ROBERT R. KIRKLAND, of Maryland, thereupon presented and read the report of the Committee on Direct Trade between Southern Atlantic Cities and Europe, including the subject of Immigration, as follows:

Your Committee from States represented in the Southern Commercial Convention meeting in Cincinnati, Ohio, October 4, 1870, to whom was referred Subject No. 1, of the Official Programme, Direct Trade between Southern Atlantic Cities and Europe, including subject of Immigration, respectfully report:

That they have given in the limited time allotted them all the attention which their paramount importance so eminently deserves.

These interests involve the restoration of American shipping, which most important question now occupies the public mind; the consideration of which the American people will require from their representatives in Congress; as it is alone to Congress we can look for relief. From them we require legislation to secure the desired results; which being accomplished, all sections of the country will be placed on an equal footing. The South will see ships, under our flag, taking off their products, and bringing in their imports, direct to their own cities; saving the varied expenses of transportation, labor, &c., &c., now involved in exports and imports through indirect ports. Under such proper arrangements, ships loaded with the products of the South would return to their own ports not only with such foreign merchandise as they require for trade and consumption, but with emigrants with large or small capital, and with sturdy muscle and energy, to settle her fertile, cheap lands and develop her resources, to the direct benefit not only of the South, but the country at large.

To accomplish these results, your Committee think that it is the true policy of the Government to grant as a bounty to all builders of ships, when registered at the respective custom houses of the country, an amount equal to all duties and taxes under the tariff and internal revenue laws, which would be paid or incurred on all articles foreign or domestic used in their construction and outfits. And further, to purchase and withdraw free from duty, from bonded warehouses at all ports where they may be, stores, supplies and outfits of every description requisite for use or consumption during their voyage (which stores and supplies on their return to a U. S. port should be placed in charge of a Government officer, not to be landed without payment of duties assessed according to law), and that all repairs and outfits from time to time required should be entitled to the same benefits proposed to be conferred above. We also recommend the enactment by Congress of a general apprenticeship law, wisely adapted to the end of supplying American seamen and officers to man and command our ships. Also to grant subsidies, in the way of mail contracts or otherwise, to lines established or to be established to the North or South of Europe or elsewhere, as their merits and services may deserve.

In the meantime, for a limited period, to allow the purchase by bona fide American citizens, in an individual or corporate capacity, of foreign built ships, to be registered and placed under the American flag, to supply the present want of American built ships, under such regulations as the practical wisdom of Congress may suggest. Our country abounds with material, wood, iron and copper, and mechanical skill ample for ship building. (Mechanics in ship building now seeking active employment in more profitable pursuits.) Capital is ready, and it only requires legislation to secure the restoration of American shipping and direct trade between Southern ports and Europe.

Accompanying the above, your Committee would report a resolution:

Resolved, That the Secretary of this Convention send copies of this report and resolution to the Representatives and Senators of the States represented in this Convention, requesting their efforts to induce Congress to pass laws in accordance with the same.

All of which is respectfully submitted.

ROBT. R. KIRKLAND, Chairman.
ROBERT S. NEWTON, Secretary.

On motion of Mr. BISHOP, of Ohio, the report was adopted as read.

Gen. N. P. BANKS, of Massachusetts, then presented and read the report of the Committee on Southern Pacific Railway, as follows:

The Committee on Southern Pacific Railway report as follows:

Resolved, That the construction of a railway from the Mississippi river to the Pacific ocean, near the 32d parallel, upon the line indicated by the Legislatures of Texas, New Mexico, Arizona and California, and substantially endorsed by the Southern Commercial Conventions held at New Orleans, Memphis and Louisville, and more recently by the State of Texas, which shall be so constructed as to connect by branches terminating at Memphis, Vicksburg and New Orleans, with the railway system of the Gulf States, and at the same time secure to all connecting roads, equal reciprocal advantages in the transmission of freight and passengers from the point of intersection with the main trunk line to the Pacific coast, is a National work of the highest importance necessary to the restoration of the commerce of the South, tending to harmonize the different sections of the country, and promote the development of its natural wealth, **and it is, therefore, eminently entitled upon every consideration of** expediency and 'public justice, to the aid from the General Government which has been so munificently extended to the Central and Northern Pacific Railways.

Respectfully submitted,
N. P. BANKS, Chairman.

On motion of Mr. BARKSDALE, of Mississippi, the report was unanimously adopted.

Gov. E. O. STANNARD, of Missouri, then presented and read the report of the Committee on River Navigation and Canals, as follows:

Your Committee respectfully report that the following subjects have been brought to their notice, by resolutions offered in the Convention, and by reports of Committees appointed at the Commercial Convention held last year at the city of Louisville:

FIRST—1. The deepening of the channel at the mouth of the Mississippi.

2. Deepening the channels of the Mississippi, Wisconsin and Arkansas rivers, and removing snags therefrom.
3. Canal at Des Moines rapids.
4. Rock Island rapids.
5. Mississippi river from Rock Island to the falls of St. Anthony.
6. Improvement of Illinois, Wisconsin and Minnesota rivers, and falls of St. Anthony.
7. Improvement of the Ohio river.
8. Louisville and Portland canal.
9. Tennessee river.
10. General surveys of various rivers.

The subjects above enumerated, have been brought before your Committee in an able and instructive report, prepared and submitted by Hon. E. O. STANNARD, Chairman of the Committee on River Navigation and Canals, appointed by the Southern Commercial Convention, held at Louisville, in October. Your Committee recommend the reading of this report before this Convention, and the adoption of the resolutions appended.

SECOND.—THE IMPROVEMENT OF THE TENNESSEE RIVER.

This subject is brought to the attention of your Committee by a special report, embodying valuable information and containing important recommendations, prepared and submitted by E. A. JAMES, Esq , Chairman of the Committee on the Improvement of the Tennessee river, appointed by the Southern Commercial Convention, held at Louisville, last October. Your Committee recommend the reading of this report also to the Convention, and the approval, by this body, of the suggestions made therein, and in this connection, also, recommend the adoption of the following :

Resolved, That the Congress of the United States be memorialized to appropriate $40,000 of the funds for the improvement of the Tennessee river, to that portion of the river between Chattanooga, Tennessee, and Knoxville, Tennessee.

THIRD.—THE IMPROVEMENT OF THE COOSA RIVER, GEORGIA.

The attention of your Committee has been called to this subject by members of the Georgia delegation, to this Convention. From their memorial it appears that the subject received the favorable consideration of the Convention at Louisville; that it is of great moment to the States of Georgia and Alabama, and has been favorably considered by the Engineer Department at Washington—official survey being made at this time under the order of the Government. Your Committee submit the following resolution for adoption by this Convention :

Resolved, That this Convention unite with the citizens of Georgia and Alabama, in recommending to Congress, an appropriation for removing obstructions in Coosa river, Alabama and Georgia, and connecting that river with the head waters of the Tennessee.

FOURTH.—THE PURCHASE OF THE ERIE CANAL FROM THE STATE OF NEW YORK, AND THE ABOLITION OF ALL TOLLS THEREON.

This resolution was submitted to the Convention by Mr. DEAKER, of New York, and referred to this Committee. Whilst recognizing the importance of the subject brought to our notice in the resolution, your Committee think the time has not yet arrived for such action as that proposed by this Convention.

FIFTH.—THE ESTABLISHMENT OF WATER COMMUNICATION BETWEEN LAKE MICHIGAN AND THE MISSISSIPPI RIVER.

The resolution upon this subject was submitted to the Convention by Mr. CHARLES SEYMOUR, of Wisconsin. Your Committee understand that a private company exists, and has received assistance for the prosecution of this work. It is now proposed, that the General Government shall purchase the interest of this company and complete the work. Its National importance justifies the Committee in recommending to the Convention the adoption of a resolution, commending the subject to the favorable consideration of Congress. Your Committee think no more specific action should be commended, without further and detailed information.

SIXTH.—THE CONNECTION OF THE ATLANTIC OCEAN AND THE GULF OF MEXICO, BY IMPROVEMENT OF VARIOUS RIVERS RUNNING ACROSS THE PENINSULA OF FLORIDA.

The resolution relating to this subject, was offered in Convention by Mr. H. L. HART, of Florida. No survey having been made of the proposed improvement, and no sufficient information being in the possession of the Committee on the subject, your Committee recommend, that the resolution offered, be filed for future action if desired.

SEVENTH.—ON THE FREE NAVIGATION OF RIVERS.

The following resolution offered by W. D. MOORE, Esq., of Pennsylvania, is recommended for adoption:

Resolved, That the free and unobstructed navigation of the rivers of the country, is the right of all its citizens, and is indispensable to the cheap transportation of its products and manufactures, and this Convention earnestly urges upon Congress the enactment of such laws, as will effectually prevent any individual or corporation from obstructing, hindering or delaying, the navigation of rivers, and from appropriating any portion of them to their own private use, or for their exclusive benefit.

EIGHTH.—THE IMPROVEMENT OF THE RED RIVER OF LOUISIANA.

This subject is brought to our attention, by resolution offered by Mr. T. P. HOTCHKISS, of Shreveport, Louisiana, and the Committee can not more strongly express their sense of the importance of the subject, and its legitimate claim upon the sympathy of your body, than by submitting for adoption the resolution included, presented by the delegate from Louisiana, as follows:

Resolved, That in the opinion of this Convention, the importance of the agricultural productions of the country bordering upon the Red river of Louisiana, deserves, at the hands of Congress, an appropriation for the removal of the raft and other obstructions to navigation in said river.

Your Committee have thus considered the important subjects referred to them, as carefully, as the time allotted to them would permit, and respectfully submit to the Convention, the foregoing report and resolutions.

        Respectfully submitted,
          E. O. STANNARD, Chairman.
W. D. MOORE, Secretary.

Mr. STANNARD, of Missouri, Chairman of the above Committee : Mr. Chairman, I also offer a report with reference to the improvement of the Tennessee river, submitted by order of the Louisville Convention:

Mr. President: I have the honor to submit the following report upon the improvement of the Tennessee river :

First—Communication from Lieut. M. B. ADAMS, Engineer U. S. A., in charge of Tennessee river improvement, marked Exhibits A and B, and made a part of this report.

It will be seen as shown by Exhibits A and B, that appropriations by Congress are sufficient to render the Tennessee river navigable, with the single exception of the obstruction at the Mussel shoals from Chattanooga, Tennessee, to Paducah, Kentucky, where the Tennessee river empties into the Ohio river.

As the Mussel shoals are the great obstruction to the free navigation of the Tennessee river, your Committee would most earnestly ask this Convention to recommend that the Congress of the United States appropriate a sufficient sum of money, to be expended under the direction of the War Department, through the Engineer Division thereof, to remove said obstructions.

Your Committee would further request that this Convention would also recommend the appropriation of sufficient money to remove the obstructions to the free navigation of the Tennessee river, between Chattanooga and Knoxville, Tennessee, and in support of which request of the Committee, we submit a few statistics marked Exhibit C.

It will be seen from Exhibits A and B, that the work heretofore ordered by acts of Congress, for the improvement of said river, has progressed rapidly, and in a short time will be completed. But the great obstructions still remain ; and hence your Committee ask that the obstructions of the Mussel shoals, and the obstructions between Chattanooga, and Knoxville, Tennessee, be removed, thereby establishing uninterrupted navigation, for 900 miles on the Tennessee river, and sixth in importance upon the American continent.

All of which is respectfully submitted,

E. A. JAMES,
Chairman Committee on Improvement of the Tennessee river,
Louisville Convention.

EXHIBIT A.

OFFICE OF THE TENN. R. IMPTS.
Chattanooga, Tenn., Sept. 6th, 1870.

Mr. E. A. JAMES, Chattanooga, Tenn.

My Dear Sir: In compliance with the verbal request you made of me some two weeks ago, I now give you in writing what I imagine to be the information you desire.

The work of improving the Tennessee river was commenced Feb. 4th, 1869; since which time the progress of the work can be seen from the "Summary Statement, &c.," enclosed herewith.

In this summary statement, the work as laid out provides for the expenditure, in the best interests of the river, and according to law, of all money appropriated for the improvement of the Tennessee river, including that of the act approved July 11th, 1870. But it will be seen that none of this goes to the improvement of Mussel shoals, that great obstruction to the navigation of the Tennessee river, though it is confidently believed that the money now appropriated is sufficient to improve the river, so that it will be navigable from Chattanooga to Decatur, and from Florence and Tuscumbia to its mouth. Very respectfully, your obt. servt.

M. B. ADAMS, 1st. Lt. U. S. Engrs.,
In charge of Tenn. R. Impts.

EXHIBIT B.

For Mr. E. A. JAMES, Chattanooga, Tenn.

SUMMARY STATEMENT OF OPERATIONS ON THE TENNESSEE RIVER IMPROVEMENTS, DURING THE YEARS 1869-70, AND PROBABLE OPERATIONS DURING THE YEAR 1870-71.

It is proposed to excavate 700 cubic yards from the Ross Towhead rock reef, and to construct a rip-rap dam with the material thus excavated.

At Tumbling shoals, $4,000 are available, and will be expended in removing loose rock from the steamboat channel.

The Suck obstruction has been very much reduced. 24,357 cubic yards have been excavated from the bar; and it is confidently believed that the work of improvement will be completed inside of two months.

There are 4,357 cubic yards remaining to be excavated, and the entire wall of excavated material is to be reveted. There has been expended on this work up to the present time, $39,637.55.

The improvement at the Pot has been reported completed, though there should still be 1,000 cubic yards taken from the projecting point which forms the obstruction; this will be done during the coming winter.

It is proposed to excavate 5,000 cubic yards from the bar at the Skillet, during the coming year.

The Widow's bar improvement will consist in the construction of a rip-rap dam to contain 1,350 cubic yards.

At Belfont shoals the same improvement is proposed as at Widow's bar.

There are two large rocks in the channel of the river near the mouth of Short creek, which will be removed during the coming year.

At Genter's reef and Genter's shoals, there are 400 cubic yards of solid rock to be excavated.

At Limestone bar, a rip-rap dam is to be constructed, that will contain 3,600 cubic yards of stone.

The Buck island rip-rap dam is complete, and contains 2,000 cubic yards of stone.

Colbert and Bee tree shoals, now in process of construction; rip-rap dams to contain a total of 12,690 cubic yards; and there are 6,448 cubic yards of solid rock to be excavated from the reefs in that vicinity.

The three last named obstructions are below Mussel shoals; all the others between Chattanooga and Decatur, in the order named.

The unusual high water of the past two months, for the season of the year, and the extreme high water during the winter and spring months, has retarded operations very much; and until the works are completed their beneficial effects can not be appreciated.

M. B. ADAMS, 1st Lt. U. S. Engineers,
In charge of Tenn. R. Improvements.

SOUTHERN COMMERCIAL CONVENTION. 59

EXHIBIT C.

STATISTICS.

Six steamers ply above Chattanooga, of from 120 to 300 tons burthen. One plies daily between Rockwood and London (mail), one runs to railroad at London, and the four largest run from Chattanooga to Kingston and Rockwood. At Rockwood are the largest iron works in the South, which will produce in 1871, 20,000 tons of pig iron and 40,000 tons of coal. In addition to the above, at Emory coal mines 10,000 tons, at Sandy coal mines 10,000 tons, and at Sole creek coal mines 10,000 tons of coal will be produced during the year 1871.

None of the foregoing is speculative, but all are in active operation now, and not doing more than one fourth of their business capacity, except the iron works at Rockwood.

It is estimated that 2,000,000 of bushels of corn are annually shipped out of Tennessee, on the river above Chattanooga; besides vast amounts of hay, flour, oats and bacon.

Flat boats now do one-third of the down stream business. 208 flat boats passed Rockwood in one week last winter, carrying freight equal to 50 trips of a 200 ton steamboat.

Millions of feet of logs come out of the upper Tennessee country annually.

Mr. STANNARD: I have the honor also to submit the following report, which the Committee recommend shall be printed:

Mr. President, in compliance with the resolution passed at the Southern Commercial Convention held in Louisville last October, requesting the chairman of each of the standing committees "to report for the respectful consideration of the next Commercial Convention upon the subject for which said committees were respectively raised," I beg leave on behalf of the Committee on River Navigation, Canals, &c., to submit for the consideration of this Convention the following report:

It will be remembered that a year ago, at Louisville, the Convention urged Congress to make an appropriation of $6,000,000, to be spent on Western waters in the completion of improvements already began and in contemplation, and in response about $2,000,000 was at the last session appropriated for these purposes, this being about the amount represented by the officers in charge of the respective works that they would require during the current year; thus showing that the West and South is no longer forgotten in the halls of Congress, and that a liberal spirit is beginning to be manifested toward us, and that earnest, urgent and intelligent appeals in our own behalf are not fruitless. That the Convention may be informed as to how this $2,000,000 was distributed, we copy the following report from the *Missouri Republican* of Western appropriations, under date of August 27th. It being the most complete of anything we have seen, and giving most thoroughly in detail the desired information.

MOUTH OF THE MISSISSIPPI.

The first important work is the deepening of the channel through the bars at the mouth of the Mississippi, for the prosecution of which during the present fiscal year, the sum of $300,000 was appropriated by the General Government. To accomplish the object the dredge boat Essayons was built, and it has now been operated for nearly two years upon Pass a l'Outre with very little success. The main difficulty which has been encountered is the frequent breaking of the machinery of the boat. The Essayons will be removed from its present field of operations at Pass a l'Outre to South-west pass, and some other step will be taken to assist in deepening the channel at this pass.

CHANNELS OF THE MISSISSIPPI, MISSOURI AND ARKANSAS.

The general improvement of the channels of the Mississippi, Missouri and Arkansas has had an appropriation made toward it of $150,000, for work during this year. The work embraces the Mississippi from New Orleans to the rapids at Keokuk. The plan of improvement is to dredge the bars at low water, remove snags, and cut down timber upon the banks at points where it would be likely to be precipitated into the river and thus form snags.

In this work four double-hull snag boats and one dredge boat are in use.

DES MOINES AND ROCK ISLAND RAPIDS.

For the construction of the canal around the Des Moines rapids at Keokuk, $600,000 has been appropriated. The canal will be 7 3-10 miles in length, 300 feet in width, and nearly 7 feet deep at extreme low water. The locks will be double, so that one boat may ascend while another is descending. It will be open for use by the fall of 1871.

There has been $150,000 appropriated for the improvement of the channel on the Rock Island rapids. The work consists in deepening the channel by blasting the rock. It will doubtless be completed before the Des Moines rapids canal.

MISSISSIPPI FROM ROCK ISLAND TO THE FALLS OF ST. ANTHONY.

The main channel of the Mississippi, from the Rock Island rapids to the Falls of St. Anthony, is being improved by the employment of tow boats which are used for the purpose of removing snags and dredging. The appropriation for the work is $60,000.

WISCONSIN, MINNESOTA AND ILLINOIS RIVERS.

The following appropriations were also made for the improvements mentioned:

Improvement of Wisconsin river	$50,000
Improvement of Minnesota river	50,000
Improvement of Illinois river	100,000
Improvement of Falls of St. Anthony	50,000

OHIO AND TENNESSEE RIVERS, AND LOUISVILLE AND PORTLAND CANAL.

For the improvement of the Ohio river, $300,000 were appropriated; $250,000 of this is for the widening and deepening of the Louisville and Portland canal at the falls. This is a most important work. It is expected that the canal will be in a condition for use within a year. The appropriation for the general improvement of the Ohio is $50,000. The Tennessee river received an appropriation of $80,000.

SURVEYS OF HARBOR OF ST. LOUIS, &C.

About $100,000 were appropriated for surveys of Western rivers, harbors of St. Louis and Alton, and some other minor works.

RECAPITULATION OF APPROPRIATIONS.

Mouth of the Mississippi	$300,000
Channels of the Mississippi, Missouri and Arkansas	150,000
Canal at Des Moines rapids	600,000
Rock Island rapids	150,000
Mississippi from Rock Island to Falls of St. Anthony	60,000
Illinois, Wisconsin and Minnesota rivers and Falls of St. Anthony	250,000
Ohio	50,000
Louisville and Portland canal	250,000
Tennessee river	80,000
Surveys (about)	100,000
Total	$1,990,000

This sum, representing these appropriations for the Mississippi and its tributaries, is about one-half of the entire appropriations made by Congress for river and harbor improvements.

It is estimated by General Wilson, the officer in charge of the canal at the Des Moines rapids, that it will cost to complete the work about $600,000, and that it can be completed during the next year, and that an appropriation of about $80,000 will complete the Rock Island rapids improvement, and that this work will be done about the same time; and by General Weitzel, the officer in charge of the Louisville canal, that to complete this work it will require an additional appropriation of about $500,000, and that the work can be completed during the year 1871.

I am informed by General Reynolds, the officer in charge of the snag boat operations on the Mississippi, Missouri and Arkansas rivers, that the appropriation of $150,000 last year for the prosecution of his work is going to be entirely inadequate for necessary expenditures during the year, and that he will ask for an appropriation of $300,000 at the next session of Congress, and an additional amount for the purchase or building of two new boats. And in view of the magnitude and importance and early completion of these great works and others to the whole country, your Committee beg to report the following preamble and resolutions for your consideration and adoption:

WHEREAS, Cheap transportation is the great want of the West, South and of the entire nation, thereby meeting the first great principles of the growth of a nation, cheap food for the masses, better remuneration for the producer, and an increase in the exports of our country; and

WHEREAS, The relative cost of transportation per mile by water and rail is as one to eight; and

WHEREAS, The Mississippi river and its tributaries affords 16,000 miles of connected navigation and the cheapest highway for the commerce of the Valley, in which is produced over two-thirds of the breadstuffs and provisions and four-fifths of the exports of the entire country; and

WHEREAS, The rate of transportation and insurance on said river and its tributaries is much increased on account of the interruption, danger and delay caused by certain obstructions; therefore,

Resolved, That the people of the United States now in convention assembled, do hereby respectfully and earnestly petition our honorable Senators and Representatives in Congress, to appropriate at their next session so much as shall be necessary to complete the improvements of the Mississippi river at the Des Moines and Rock Island rapids, the completion of the Louisville and Portland canal at the falls of the Ohio, and the deepening of the channel at the mouth of the Mississippi.

Resolved, That fully appreciating the work now being done at the Balize, at the mouth of the Mississippi river, and the removal of snags and dredging of sand bars on the lower Mississippi, the Missouri and Arkansas rivers, and the falls at Alexandria on Red river, and on the upper Mississippi, Wisconsin and Minnesota rivers, and the removal of obstructions to navigation of the Tennessee, Ohio and Illinois rivers, we do most earnestly and respectfully request Congress to appropriate at their next session so much as can be judiciously expended on the continued improvement of the navigation on said rivers.

Resolved, That the thanks of the people of the Mississippi valley are due and are hereby cordially tendered to the Thirty-ninth, Fortieth, Forty-first and Forty-second Congress, for appropriations granted by them for the improvement of the Western rivers, and especially to those members whose warm sympathy and earnest labor contributed so largely to secure such appropriations.

Respectfully yours,
E. O. STANNARD.

A protracted discussion ensued, upon the motion of Mr. GASKELL, of Georgia, to adopt the reports and resolutions as submitted by the Committee.

Gen. CHILTON, of Kentucky, demanded the vote on the motion by States.

The call resulted as follows:

Yeas—Alabama 8, Arkansas 4, Florida 3, Georgia 12, Iowa 1, Kansas 3, Louisiana 8, Mississippi 7, Missouri 10, Massachusetts 1, Ohio 21, Pennsylvania 4, South Carolina 6, Tennessee 8, Texas 1, Virginia 10, Nevada 1. Total, 108.

Nays- Kentucky 11, Maryland 7, Michigan 8, New York 6, North Carolina 2, Tennessee 1. Total, 35.

The report was declared adopted by a vote of 108 to 35.

Gen. CLINTON B. FISK, of Missouri, then presented and read the report of the Committee on Removal of Obstructions from the Mouth of the Mississippi river, as follows:

To the Southern Commercial. Convention, Cincinnati, Ohio:

Your Committee to whom was referred the subject of removing the obstructions from the mouth of the Mississippi river, having had the same under consideration, would respectfully report, that the Committee appointed at the Louisville Convention in October, 1869, have carefully watched the progress made by the United States government steamer Essayons in opening and maintaining channels at the river's mouth. The results are not such as to warrant the belief that permanent channels can be maintained through such instrumentality.

The Essayons has during the last year been much of the time in docks for repairs, and is at this time undergoing reconstruction. New machinery is being added, and she will soon be ready for another trial. But should any serious accident happen to her machinery, or the channels again be filled by the violence of the storms to which the gulf coast is subject, the commerce of the Mississippi valley would suffer a loss of many millions of dollars.

Your Committee believe that no subject within the range of the discussions of this Convention is fraught with greater interest to the entire country than is this.

The Mississippi river and its tributaries drain more than half of the territorial area of the United States. This area is pervaded in every part by lands of unsurpassed fertility, a comparatively small portion of which is yet developed. It supports within its bounds a majority of the population of the Union. It pays more than half the taxes of the entire country. Taken altogether, in soil, production, mineral wealth and navigable waters, this great valley far surpasses any other on the face of the globe, and is destined at no very distant day to exert a controlling influence upon the policy of the Government. The interests of the people of every part of this valley in the removal of impediments from the navigable streams, and deepening the channels of the mouths of the Mississippi, are identical, and these objects ought to be provided by the aid of the General Government to the largest extent, as the best means of securing the prosperity of the whole country, promoting the happiness of the people, insuring peace, concord and unity at home, and respect and renown abroad.

We commend to the Southern Commercial Convention, composed as it is of delegates from all the States of this great valley, and from a large number of other States of the Union, the adoption of resolutions earnestly urging upon the National Government the necessity of deepening, in the most expeditious manner possible, both channels at the mouths of the Mississippi river to a depth that shall at all times pass vessels of at least twenty feet draught. Therefore, be it

Resolved, That all obstructions to navigation at the mouth of the Mississippi river, should be removed at the expense, and under the direction of the government.

1. By a continued and conclusive experiment to be made by dredging, or

2. That the Government of the United States shall, (if the same be found practicable by a preliminary survey,) open a ship canal from a point on the left bank of the Mississippi river, below Fort St. Phillip, into the Gulf of Mexico—such canal to be constructed and maintained at National cost, and administered by National authority : to be adequate to the wants of American commerce—free from any charge or impediment, and to constitute a part of the National highway to the ocean.

Resolved, That a Special Committee, consisting of one member from each of the following cities, to wit: New Orleans, Vicksburg, Memphis, Cairo, St. Louis, Keokuk, Dubuque, St. Paul, Louisville, Cincinnati and Pittsburg, be appointed by the President of this Convention, whose duty it shall be to confer with the government authorities, respecting the prosecution of the work of deepening the channel of the river mouth, by the present agencies or other new appliances—the survey for a ship canal, and to awaken a general interest in the much needed National work, among the people of the Mississippi valley.

Your Committee append as a part of their report, communications from BENJAMIN BURISON, the venerable and respected ex-engineer of the State of Louisiana, and Captain C. W. HOWELL, an able officer of the Engineer corps of the United States army, now in charge of the steamer Essayons, and other documents respecting surveys and construction of a ship canal connecting the Mississippi river with the gulf of Mexico, through Isle Breton pass.

All of which is respectfully submitted,

CLINTON B. FISK, Chairman of Com.

L. J. HIGBY, Sec.

ENGINEER'S OFFICE,
New Orleans, Sept. 30, 1870.
L. J. HIGBY, Esq.

Dear Sir: In 1836, I surveyed the coast of the gulf from above Fort St. Philip, down to the passes of the river, and found by observation and sounding, that no deposits of the Mississippi mud were made on that coast, or by the gulf stream, east of the passes; but found the sediment all went to the westward by the action of the gulf stream and the current of the Mississippi.

In the year 1840, I went with Commodore Rousseau, in command of a U. S. corvette to make a reconnoissance of the aforesaid coast, and came to anchor near the shore, five miles below Fort St. Philip, in Breton Island pass. I found five to eight and ten fathoms water out the pass, and I have no doubt, a ship canal with twenty-five or thirty feet water can be built there; and from my experience, I am satisfied no deposit will ever be made at the outward end of the canal to form any bar.

Any other information you may want, I will be happy to give.

Very respectfully yours,
BENJAMIN BURISON, Civil Engineer.

U. S. ENGINEER'S OFFICE,
New Orleans, Sept. 25, 1870.
L. J. HIGBY, Esq.

Dear Sir: In complying with your request for an expression of opinion regarding a project for a ship canal, below Fort St. Philip, connecting the Mississippi river with the gulf of Mexico, through Isle Breton pass. I have first to say, that like yourself, I have only the evidence of others on which to base my opinions, not having as yet made a personal examination of the proposed location.

The subject was brought officially to my notice by the Engineer Department, last July, and having previously paid some attention to it, I was able on the 12th August, to report the project "apparently practicable, and its realization of the greatest moment to the commerce of the Mississippi." Reserving further report until after making an examination of Isle Breton pass, which I intend to make as soon as more pressing duties will permit.

Of objections to the project, which I have considered, but one is of a serious nature, all others regard difficulties to be overcome by the engineer. The one is the asserted continuous shoaling of Isle Breton pass, and of the bay and sound to the northward, from natural causes, which shoaling, if as asserted, would eventually effect a blockade of the outer end of any canal debouching into Isle Breton pass.

Such evidence as we now have shows that no such shoaling has taken place within the past one hundred years, but that, on the contrary, the pass has actually deepened. Without calling in question the correctness of this evidence, I am yet of opinion that it should be verified by soundings of later date than those we have, before presenting the project to Congress for definite action. Such soundings can be obtained in time to present to Congress at its next session, and will be found in a report I shall make in November, to the Chief Engineer, U. S. A. Assuming the depth of the pass not naturally subject to diminution, the construction of this projected canal, will involve but a single problem requiring more than ordinary engineering ability, namely: the projection of its debouché into the deep water of the pass, in such a manner as not to cause shoaling, by obstructing the currents, (tidal or others) through the pass.

The work of excavation will be of the simplest and least expensive character, and there is no question as to finding or making proper foundations for locks and other structures.

A review of the estimates made by Mr. R. MONTAGUE, C. E., and published in 1869, satisfies me that they are too small. I have not had time to review them. Of this plan I have only to suggest that the width of water way should at least be doubled.

However successful the work now in progress, for improving channels across the bars at the mouth of the Mississippi may prove, a canal such as the one projected, will yet be of incalculable benefit to the commerce of that river—a commerce destined to equal that of New York.

I am, sir, very respectfully, your obedient servant,

C. W. HOWELL,
Capt. Topog'rs. U. S. A.

The report and resolutions were adopted.

Mr. BRANCH, of Virginia, presented and read a partial report of the Committee on Finance and Taxation, as follows:

Your Committee fully recognize the importance and magnitude of the topics which have been referred to them, and that they may be the better able to discharge the duties assigned them, beg leave at this time to submit a report covering only a part of the subject matter of their investigations, and at the same time ask for further time to prepare an additional report.

Upon the subject of tariff, they recommend the adoption of the following:

Resolved. That we are in favor of a tariff for purposes of revenue only.

That duties should never be levied with a view to give one branch of industry, or one section of the country an advantage over others; that the rates should be fixed with regard solely to revenue, and should be made to bear as lightly as possible on all branches of industry, and upon all sections of the country.

Upon the subject of internal revenue taxation, your Committee recommend that the system be further amended by the entire abolition of the income tax, taxation be restricted to articles of luxury, and that their number be as small as may be compatible with the amount of revenue to be raised.

Mr. JEWETT, of Missouri, announced that the report as presented by Mr. BRANCH, did not meet with the endorsement of the entire Committee, and that the minority of the Committee had thought of also presenting a report, but after consideration, decided that it was not necessary to do so.

On motion of Mr. JEWETT, the consideration of the report was deferred until the full and final report of the Committee was submitted.

Mr. W. T. NEWMAN, of Georgia, Chairman of Committee on The Enlargement of the more important Lines of Canals in the United States, so as to render them navigable for Vessels propelled by Steam, then presented and read the report of that Committee, as follows:

Mr. Chairman: The Committee appointed to consider the enlargement of the more important lines of canals in the United States, so as to render them navigable for vessels propelled by steam, in view of the very great pressure of business before the Convention, recommend that the subject submitted to them, be continued until the next session of the Convention.

Which was unanimously adopted.

Mr. JOHN G. FOX, of Nevada, then presented and read the report of the Committee on the Charges on Passenger and Freight Traffic on Rail and Water Lines, as follows:

The Committee on the Charges on Passenger and Freight Traffic on Railroad and Water Lines, respectfully report the following resolution, and recommend its adoption:

Resolved, That Congress be invoked to pass such laws as may be deemed necessary to establish a fair and equitable schedule of rates for freight and passenger transportation, without discrimination against local traffic, on all roads endowed by government, either by grants of land or money, and that the same action be invoked by State Legislatures, with reference to roads under their control.

Which was unanimously adopted.

Mr. Wm. S. HASTIE, of South Carolina, presented and read the report of the Committee on subject No. 13.—To abolish throughout the whole country all license imposed on Commercial Travelers, as follows:

The Committee to whom was referred the subject To abolish throughout the whole country, all license imposed on Commercial Travelers, beg leave to report, that after a long discussion, the vote resulted in a tie, and the Committee throw the whole matter in the hands of the Convention, without any recommendation.

On motion, the report was laid on the table.

The Committee on Free Trade in Money reported through its chairman, Mr. CHARLES REEMELIN, of Ohio, the following resolution, viz:

Resolved, That all restrictions upon the rates of interest, they being but the price of money, serve to increase rather than to diminish its cost; that to bring the rate of interest to the lowest practical standard, the trade in money should be left as free as the trade in merchandise, and this Convention recommends to the several States the repeal of all usury laws and of all statutes by which contracts expressed in money are treated exceptionally.

Resolved, That the banking laws of the country should be so amended as to take from them all monopoly in the supply of currency or other forms of credit for the wants of business, and so as to allow every person the free use of his credit.

Resolved, That the free use of their means and their credit is the natural right of all human beings, and no government has the right to interfere with this freedom, except where fraud or crime enters into the transaction and is duly proven in a court of justice.

The motion to adopt the resolutions occasioned a lengthy discussion, resulting in their passage, but on motion of Mr. WICKERSHAM, of Alabama, the vote adopting them was reconsidered, and the further consideration of the subject postponed until the afternoon session of the Convention.

Mr. FLUELLEN, of Georgia, by general consent, offered the following:

Resolved, That the Southern Commercial Convention respectfully recommend that the United States Congress donate or appropriate certain lands for railroad purposes, to each of the Southern States, and to locate said lands in some of the Territories. That these lands shall be sold at stated times by State authority, and never less than at the price of United States public lands in the same sections of country.

Which was referred to the Committee on the subject of a Settled Policy in regard to the Disposition of the Public Lands.

Mr. CAMPBELL, of North Carolina, by general consent, offered the following:

WHEREAS, The State of North Carolina ceded to the United States the territory now forming the State of Tennessee, an area of land surpassing in excellence and richness that derived from any other source, except the North-west Territory, ceded by Virginia; and

WHEREAS, One of the great highways from the Southern Pacific Railroad to the middle East lies through her mountain lands; therefore

Resolved, That we recommend the passage by the United States Congress of a liberal appropriation to the Transatlantic Western North Carolina Railroad.

Which was referred to the Committee on Railroads Generally.

Mr. DORN, of Kentucky, by general consent, offered the following:

Resolved, That the proposed connection of the Atlantic and Pacific waters by means of the Darien canal, is of the greatest importance to American trade and commerce, and should be the work of American energy, American talent, and American money; and we do most respectfully ask of the Congress of the United States all legitimate aid, and its fostering care, to this great American project.

Which was adopted.

The Convention then, on motion, adjourned until 3 o'clock, P. M.

AFTERNOON SESSION.

The Convention was called to order at 3 P. M., Mr. GARRETT presiding.

Mr. CORWINE, of Ohio, arose to a question of privilege, and said:

Mr. President, since the adjournment of this Convention last evening, and during its session this morning, a member of this Convention, a delegate, has died. Died suddenly. Died in the midst of life, and in the midst of usefulness. Died under circumstances of peculiar distress to his friends. Mr. GEORGE L. JOHNSON, a delegate representing the Board of Trade of Cincinnati in this Convention, fell dead this morning of heart disease. The Ohio delegation, who have directed me to announce this melancholy event to this Convention, desire me to say of him that he was a man of irreproachable character and integrity, and he had promise of a future alike creditable to himself and the city in which he lived.

Mr. Chairman, I beg to add one remark. I knew him when he was a boy. I knew him on the soil of Kentucky. I knew him there as a boy who gave great promise of future usefulness in this life which has suddenly come to an end, regretted by me and regretted by the community.

The President of the Convention said:

The Chair fully appreciates the circumstances of the melancholy announcement made by the gentleman from Ohio, and extends the heartfelt sympathy of the Convention to the friends and family of the deceased.

Mr. R. M. Bishop, of Cincinnati, offered the following resolution by consent of the Convention:

Resolved, That the official reporter of this Convention be requested to furnish a full report of the remarks of Mr. Corwine, of Ohio, and the President of this Convention, in respect to the death of George L. Johnson, a delegate to the Convention, and that the same be sent to the widow and family of the deceased.

The rules were suspended, and the resolution was unanimously adopted by the Convention.

Mr. Fisk, of Missouri, by general consent, offered the following:

Resolved, That the interest of the South and of the whole country will be promoted by the early completion of the Atlantic & Pacific Railroad, and to that end we urge the subject upon the consideration of Congress, earnestly recommending that such further legislation be granted to that road as will enable the company to complete it at the earliest possible time through the Territories of the United States.

Adopted.

The Chair announced the following as the special committee provided for in the report of the Committee on the Removal of Obstructions from the Mouth of the Mississippi:

L. J. Higby, New Orleans; R. S. Buck, Vicksburg; Jacob Thompson, Memphis; W. P. Halliday, Cairo; Clinton B. Fisk, St. Louis; R. F. Bower, Keokuk; H. Lowry, Dubuque; D. W. Ingersoll, St. Paul; James Bridgeford, Louisville; Theo. Cook, Cincinnati; W. D. Moore, Pittsburg.

Also the following special committee appointed under resolution of the Convention, of one member from each State. represented, to fix a time and place for the next session of the Convention, and to report a basis of representation thereto:

H. N. Snyder, Tennessee; Theodore Cook, Ohio; M. D. Wickersham, Alabama; George E. Dodge, Arkansas; P. H. Raiford, Florida; R. L. Mott, Georgia; Thos. M. Munroe, Iowa; P. L. Underwood, Illinois; W. R. Bowes, Indiana; Wm. Ernst, Kentucky;

Col. Coffin, Kansas; John H. Kennard, Louisiana; E. Stafford, Mississippi; R. T. Kirkland, Maryland; Gen. Clinton B. Fisk, Missouri; Wm. A. Butler, Michigan; Gen. N. P. Banks, Massachusetts; Peter Clark, New York; J. G. Fox, Nevada; A. A. Campbell, North Carolina; W. D. Moore, Pennsylvania; J. B. Cohen, South Carolina; Gov. J. W. Throckmorton, Texas; Col. Thos. Branch, Virginia; Charles Seymour, Wisconsin; Jesse B. Wilson, District of Columbia.

The Chair announced that the consideration of the resolutions presented by the Committee on Free Trade in Money would now be in order.

After a motion of Mr. STYLES, of Georgia, to lay the resolutions on the table, and a motion of Mr. JAMES, of Tennessee, for the previous question, were lost, Mr. BISHOP, of Ohio, demanded a separate vote on each of the three resolutions, which was sustained.

The first resolution was then adopted; after a lengthy discussion the second resolution was lost, and the third resolution was laid on the table.

Mr. R. M. BISHOP, of Ohio, presented and read the report of the Committee on a Settled Policy in the Public Interest in regard to the Disposition of Government Lands, as follows:

Resolved, That it should be the settled policy of the United States to regard the public lands not as capital or a source of revenue, but as a means of increasing the population and enlarging the wealth of the country; and to this end the homestead law should be sustained; and in regions where the settlement of the country is necessary to give value to the lands and promote the interests of the people, such appropriations of alternate sections as may be necessary to secure these objects must be considered beneficent and wise. But the public interest imperatively demands that such lands, whether reserved by the Government or appropriated to aid public improvements, should be held for the benefit of actual settlers at an average price not exceeding $2.50 an acre; and every appropriation of public lands for these purposes should be accompanied by such limitations, restrictions and conditions as will compel corporations or other grantees, under penalty of forfeiture, to seek their profit by promoting the settlement of the country instead of speculating in the lands intrusted to them; secure the prompt construction of the public works in aid of which they are appropriated; and protect to the fullest extent the interests of the Government and the right of actual settlers.

Resolved, That a committee of three be appointed by the Chair to memorialize Congress upon this subject, setting forth the views entertained by this Convention.

The report was unanimously adopted.

Col. M. A. BRYSON, of Missouri, then presented and read the report of the Committee on Wharfage on Navigable Rivers, as follows:

Your Committee beg leave to report the following facts and conclusions:

The charges upon the tonnage of the Western rivers by the different municipalities, under the title of wharfage, are exorbitant, operating seriously as a burden upon commerce. For instance, the charges at the city of Cincinnati are 9 cents, at the city of St. Louis, 7 cents, at the city of Memphis 6 cents, and at the city of New Orleans 10 cents per ton, on the carrying capacity of every boat, for the privilege of touching at its public landing.

And, in addition, nearly every village of a few houses, although no improvements may have been made at its public landing, makes some charge for the same privilege.

So great is the aggregation of these charges, that each boat pays under the name of wharfage from 15 to 30 cents for every ton of freight she carries.

Your Committeee would also state, they believe such a tonnage tax to be specially prohibited by the 10th Section of the 1st Article of the Constitution of the United States, which prohibits any State, and thereby any city receiving its authority to tax, from the State, from imposing any tonnage tax.

Your Committee believe further, that what are known as wharves upon these rivers, partake as much of the character of streets as wharves, and in equity the expense of maintaining the same, should be borne by the city and the boat equally. But finding, as we do, that the charges imposed are from five to ten times the amount actually necessary to keep the wharves in repair, we would most respectfully ask the various municipalities to remove this charge, or to reduce it to an equitable sum. And in the event of their failing or refusing to do so, that under its constitutional power of regulating commerce between the different States, Congress be requested to pass such laws as will prohibit, and protect against unreasonable charges.

A motion to recommit the report to the Committee was lost, and after a very lengthy discussion the report was adopted, under a call for the previous question.

Hon. E. A. JAMES, of Tennessee, presented and read the report of the Committee on Ample Railroad Facilities from the Ohio river to the Central South, as follows:

Your Committee, (No. 18,) on Ample Railroad Facilities from the Ohio river to the Central South, beg leave to present the following report of preambles and resolutions, unanimously adopted by your Committee, and which we hope will meet the like approbation of this Convention, to wit:

WHEREAS, Railroads tend to increase production, consumption, and the general development of the resources of the country through which they may pass, thereby augmenting the general prosperity and wealth of the whole country; and

WHEREAS, There are no direct railroads running from the Ohio river to the Central South, through a large portion of the great States of Kentucky, Virginia, North Carolina, Georgia, Alabama and Tennessee, to the harbors of the Atlantic and Gulf coasts, including that great belt of country lying between the 3d and 8th meridian, West longitude, from Washington, abounding in agricultural and mineral wealth, as yet almost entirely undeveloped; therefore,

1st. *Be it resolved,* That this Convention recommend most earnestly to the favorable consideration of the Legislatures of the different States, and also to the counties and municipal corporation authorities through which they may pass and terminate, the following projected lines of railways, and respectfully ask that liberal legislation be granted, and a generous support extended said lines by those whom they will directly benefit, as well as for the general benefit that will be derived therefrom by the country at large. Said roads which your Committee specially recommend for the approval of this Convention, are the following, to wit:

1. The Cincinnati Southern Railroad.
2. The Louisville & Chattanooga Grand Trunk Railroad.
3. The Cumberland & Ohio Railroad.

2d. *Be it further resolved*, That this Convention urges upon the General Assembly of the State of Kentucky, the necessity of granting a charter to the Cincinnati Southern Railroad, from Cincinnati to Chattanooga, or to such other point South as may be deemed advisable by the trustees or corporators, and that the line should be as direct as practicable.

Which was adopted.

Mr. JAMES also presented the following supplemental report of the Committee:

WHEREAS, There exists State charters for a railroad from St. Louis, Missouri, to Mt. Carmel, Illinois, via New Albany, Indiana, thence to Louisville, Kentucky, thence through Pound Gap to Wythville, West Virginia, and thence to Norfolk, Virginia, making a continuous Air Line from Norfolk, Virginia, to St. Louis, Missouri; therefore,

1st. *Be it resolved*, That this Convention recommend to the United States Congress, the granting of a National railroad charter over the routes above named from Norfolk, Virginia, to St. Louis, Missouri, to be known as the Norfolk, Louisville & St. Louis Air Line Railroad.

2d. *Be it further resolved*, That the Senators and Representatives in Congress, of the States interested in said railroad, be and they are hereby requested to bring this subject before Congress, in order to procure such legislation as the importance of said contemplated road demands, and should receive.

Mr. WRIGHTSON, of Kentucky, said that this same subject had been on his own motion, decided once by the Memphis Convention, as belonging to the debatable ground between the legislative powers of Congress and the reserved rights of the States. He therefore moved to lay the supplemental report on the table.

On this question a division was ordered.

During the discussion which followed, Mr. CHILTON, of Kentucky, offered the following amendment to the report:

Resolved, That while this Convention deems it proper, and is willing to recommend and urge the granting of facilities and encouragement to all railroad enterprises, it does not recognize the right of the Federal Government to grant Federal charters of railroads through States, except to such companies as may have first obtained charters from the State authorities through which the proposed line of railway may pass, and who are subject to the local civil authorities for the management and conduct of the affairs thereof.

Which created a lengthy and sectional debate,—to end which Mr. CHILTON withdrew the amendment.

The vote upon laying the report on the table under the call for a division, was decided carried.

Mr. WRIGHTSON then gave notice to the Convention that he would on the following day, at the special request of the Louisville delegation, move a reconsideration of the vote by which the report was laid on the table.

A communication was received from the officers of the Georgia State Fair, in session at Atlanta, Georgia, containing an invitation to the members of the Convention to attend the Fair, which was read and ordered filed.

The Committee on Reciprocal Trade between the United States and Brazil and other South American countries, reported the following:

Resolved, That the great importance of the subject of the encouragement and building up of a reciprocal trade between the United States and Brazil and other South American States, demands the careful consideration of Congress, and to the end that the advantages to accrue therefrom to our country, may be more fully impressed upon the National Legislature, the Hons. PETER CLARK, of New York; THOS. C. FLETCHER, of Missouri, and Mr. BURWELL, of Louisiana, be authorized to prepare a memorial on this subject, for presentation to Congress at its next session.

Which was unanimously adopted.

Mr. SNYDER, of Tennessee, by leave, offered the following:

Resolved, That a direct central line of water communication between the North and South, is of vital importance to the commercial interests of the country, as well as a means of National unity and National security, and that such a line is afforded by way of the Ohio, Tennessee, Coosa and Alabama rivers, and a canal connecting the Coosa and Tennessee rivers.

Resolved, That such legislation, both State and National, as will secure the opening of this line is recommended by this Convention.

Resolved, That this enterprise is as much deserving of appropriations to aid in carrying it forward, as any enterprise that has received assistance.

Which, on motion of the same gentleman, were referred to a special committee of five, to be appointed by the Chair.

The Chair announced as the special committee to whom the resolutions of Mr. SNYDER would be referred, the following:

H. N. Snyder, Tennessee; M. D. Wickersham, Alabama; R. L. Mott, Georgia; A. S. Berry, Kentucky; C. W. Rowland, Ohio.

Mr. THOS. R. BIGGS, of Ohio, presented and read the report of the Committee on Tares and Short Weights, as follows:

The Committee to whom was referred the subject of Tares and Short Weights, after full consideration, have agreed to recommend the following resolution as their report:

Resolved, That the constituent bodies represented in this Convention, be requested to advocate the adoption of a rule, that Tares in all transactions, should be the actual weight of the package at the time of sale; and to insist upon full weight and measure in articles purporting to be of a certain fixed standard, but which is sold by the parcel or package.

All of which is respectfully submitted.

Which was unanimously adopted.

The Committee upon the Removal of the National Capital being called,

Mr. FORSHEY, of Texas, said: Mr. President, that Committee has no report to make. (Applause.)

Mr. ABLE of Missouri, presented and read the report of

the Committee on Obstruction to Navigation by Narrow Span Bridge Piers, as follows:

To the Southern Commercial Convention:

Your Committee appointed to report on Obstructions to Navigation by Narrow Span Bridge Piers, would respectfully report: That there seems an urgent and pressing necessity for such legislation on the part of Congress, in regard to bridging the Mississippi, Missouri, Ohio and their tributaries, and all other navigable rivers, by the enactment of a law, that will so regulate the construction of bridges, as to secure navigation from needless obstruction, and at the same time, afford every reasonable facility for railroad and common traffic across their streams.

It has been demonstrated, both in this country and in Europe, that such bridges can be constructed, and that the length of span or hight of bridge, in crossing a stream, is merely a question of cost—and we think, such legislation on the part of our Government, as permits the utility of these rivers as channels of commerce, to be impaired merely to save a portion of the cost of erecting bridges across them, ill advised—and demanding such supervision on the part of the General Government, as will secure the prior vested rights in their natural channels of commerce, to all her citizens. It is undoubtedly true, that most of the bridges now spaning Western navigable rivers, needlessly retard and impede commerce, and many of those now in process of building, or to be built under charters granted or supposed to be granted by Congress, will if permitted to be completed under their present plans and specifications as to hight of bridge above high water mark, and width of span across the channel, render these rivers useless and worthless to the people of this country, for the purposes of transportation.

It is needless for this Committee to call the attention of this Convention, to the vast amount in tonnage and the value of the agricultural, mineral and manufactured products, now transported with great facility and cheapness, on their natural highways of commerce.

We are satisfied that the increased risks resulting from these artificial obstructions, enhancing the cost of insurance, and the direct losses they have occasioned each year, to the commerce of these rivers, would more than defray the cost of proper bridges.

We would therefore earnestly recommend the immediate attention of Congress to this subject; and respectfully suggest the enactment of a law substantially the same as that contained in a bill which passed one branch of Congress at its last session, entitled "A bill to authorize the construction of bridges across the Mississippi river and the Missouri river, and the Ohio river," which bill is hereunto annexed, and respectfully submitted as a part of this report:

BRIDGE BILL.

A BILL TO AUTHORIZE THE CONSTRUCTION OF BRIDGES ACROSS THE MISSISSIPPI RIVER, THE MISSOURI RIVER, AND THE OHIO RIVER.

Be it enacted by the Senate and House of Representatives of the United States of America, in Congress assembled, That any bridge hereafter erected across the Ohio river, shall be made with continuous or unbroken spans, and the span across the main low water channel shall not be of less elevation than 90 feet above low water mark, nor less than 40 feet above extreme high water mark, as understood at the points of location, measuring for such elevation to the bottom chord of the bridge. All the spans, other than the one over the main low water channel, shall be at least 300 feet in length, in the clear, and the span covering the main low water channel of the river shall be of such length as to leave at least 400 feet of unobstructed passage-way for navigation at all stages.

SEC. 2. That any bridge built under the provisions of this act shall be located at such places and in such manner as to be at right angles with the direction of the current in the main channel of the river at all stages, so that the piers of said bridge may always be parallel to the current in the main channel; and the location of the bridge shall also be such that the current of the main channel shall move in a straight line from a point at least 1,500 feet above the bridge, to a point 500 feet below the bridge, and no rip-rap or other material shall be placed around the bases of the piers or abutments to compensate for inadequate foundations, which material shall contract the passage-way hereinbefore provided, or which shall injuriously affect the regimen of the river.

SEC. 3. That any person, company or corporation authorized to construct a bridge across the Ohio river by the States upon whose territory said bridge will abut, shall submit to the Secretary of War, for his examination, a design of the bridge and piers, and a map of the location, giving for the space of at least one mile above and one mile below the proposed location, the topography of the banks of the river, the shore lines at high and low water, the direction of the current at all stages, and the soundings, accurately showing the bed of the stream, and shall furnish such other information as may be required for a full and satisfactory understanding of the subject by the Secretary of War; and if the Secretary of War is satisfied that the provisions of the law have been complied with in regard to location, the building of piers may be at once commenced; but if it shall appear that the conditions prescribed by this act can not be complied with at the location where it is desired to construct the bridge, the Secretary of War shall detail a board, composed of three experienced officers of the corps of engineers, to examine the case, and may, on their recommendation, authorize the building of the bridge, at the proposed location, on such increased length of spans across the channel way, as the board may deem sufficient to secure a passage-way that shall not unnecessarily obstruct the navigation of the river.

SEC. 4. That any person, company or corporation constructing a bridge under this act shall take all necessary measures to prevent any change occurring in the river bed, after the work shall have been completed, that would injuriously affect the navigation of the river, and shall not, during the construction of the bridge, obstruct the navigation of the river in any way that will not at all times leave a passage-way equivalent to that heretofore provided in this act.

SEC 5. That any bridge constructed under this act, and according to its limitations, shall be a lawful structure, and shall be recognized and known as a post route, upon which also no higher charge shall be made for the transmission over the same of the mails, the troops and the munitions of war of the United States than the rate per mile paid for their transportation over the railroads or public highways leading to said bridge; and in case of any litigation arising from any obstructions or alleged obstruction to the navigation of said river, created by the construction of any bridge under this act, the cause or question arising may be tried before the District Court of the United States, or any State in which any portion of said obstruction or bridge touches.

SEC. 6. That all bridges hereafter to be built on the Mississippi, below the mouth of the Missouri, shall be constructed under the foregoing conditions and restrictions, with the exception that the main span shall be at least 500 feet in the clear.

SEC. 7. That all bridges hereafter built on the Missouri river and Mississippi river, above the mouth of the Missouri, shall be built **under the foregoing conditions and restrictions**, with the following exceptions, viz: If constructed with continuous spans, said bridge shall have one span over the main channel of not less than 300 feet clear water way, and the bottom chord of said bridge shall be not less than 50 feet above extreme high water mark ; and if built as a draw bridge, it may be constructed with a pivot or counter-balance draw over the main channel of not less than 300 feet clear water ; and that the draw shall be promptly opened upon signal, that no delay be caused to any steamboat, or barge tow, or other craft.

SEC. 8. That the right to alter or amend this act so as to prevent or remove all material obstructions to the navigation of said river by the construction of bridges, is hereby expressly reserved.

Which was adopted.

Mr. STEWART, of Alabama, presented and read the report of the Committee on the subject to Abolish all Toll Charges on the Navigable Rivers of the United States, as follows:

In the absence of the action of former Commercial Conventions, if any has been had, on the subject of tolls on the navigable rivers of the United States, your Committee would respectfully and unanimously submit the following:

WHEREAS, In the opinion of this Convention the benefits of the General Government should be distributed and conferred equally upon all portions of the country, and all its citizens ; and

WHEREAS, The Government has very judiciously and beneficially appropriated money for the improvement of its rivers and harbors, a liberal continuation of which this Convention earnestly recommends ; and

WHEREAS, The benefits and improvements from such appropriations have been made free, with the exception of the Louisville and Portland canal ; it is therefore

Resolved, That this Convention respectfully urge upon Congress, at its next session, the prompt appropriation of money sufficient for the immediate completion of the enlargement of said Louisville and Portland canal, now in process of enlargement, and at once make it free to all the various commerce of the country.

Resolved, That the present unfinished canal around the Mussel shoals in the Tennessee river, be purchased by the General Government, and sufficient money appropriated for the enlargement of the same, to meet the wants of the rapidly growing commerce of the vast country watered by the Tennessee and its tributaries; and that the same be made free of toll.

Resolved, That this Convention is opposed to the collection of tolls upon any of our navigable rivers, and respectfully recommends to Congress to make free the improvements on the same, which have been or may be made, from moneys appropriated by the General Government.

Resolved, That as our navigable rivers will ever constitute one of the great arteries of commerce, and are therefore worthy of especial attention in consideration of the facilities they afford for the interchange of commodities, every scheme that contemplates their obstruction, or in any degree renders their navigation more expensive or dangerous, should be vigorously opposed, and defeated at all hazards, and unceasing efforts should be especially directed to remove every obstruction that now exists to their free and economical use as the highways for the commerce of the whole country.

Which was adopted.

The presentation and consideration of the report of the Committee on Enlargement of the more important Lines of Canals in the United States, so as to render them Navigable by Vessels propelled by Steam, was, on motion, postponed until the next session of the Convention.

Mr. COLE, of Tennessee, offered the following:

Resolved, That all breaks and obstructions in our great highways of trade and travel be remedied, and the connection of tracks and uniformity of gauge be perfected as early as possible, so that trains may pass from one road to another without annoyance or delay to either passengers or freight.

Which was referred to the Committee on Railroads Generally.

The Committee on Charges on Passenger and Freight Traffic by Rail and Water Lines, presented the following:

A BILL

TO BE ENTITLED: AN ACT TO AUTHORIZE SUBSCRIPTION BY THE UNITED STATES IN AID OF THE CONSTRUCTION OF RAILROADS, AND TO REGULATE THE RATES TO BE CHARGED FOR TRANSPORTATION THEREON.

SECTION 1. *Be it enacted by the Senate and House of Representatives of the United States, in Congress assembled,* That there shall be, and is hereby created, a Supervisory Board, to consist of the Secretary of the Treasury, the Secretary of War, the Postmaster-General, the Attorney-General, the Commissary-General, the Quartermaster General and the Comptroller of the Currency, who shall be *ex-officio* members thereof; and that when any railroad company, which now is or may hereafter be organized under a charter granted by any State or Territory of the United States, shall adduce to them satisfactory proof that they have a *bona fide* subscription for a sum equal to seventy-five per cent. of the cost of the construction and equipment of their road, and that the payment thereof, in national currency, or in specie within thirty years thereafter, with interest, at the rate of four per cent. per annum, payable semi-annually, has been satisfactorily secured by a pledge of bonds and mortgages of real estate, or by other good and approved securities, and shall ask a subscription on the part of the United States. Then it shall be the duty of the said Board to submit to Congress a report, embracing a copy of their charter, the estimated cost of the construction and equipment of their road, the report of the engineer-in chief, by whom the surveys and estimates have been made, the amount of subscriptions, and the guarantee by which payment has been secured; and if Congress shall by resolution, assent, then it shall be the duty of the Secretary of the Treasury, in the name of and for the United States, to subscribe for and on account of the United States, for shares of such company, the par of which shall be equal to twenty-five per cent. of the estimated cost of the construction and equipment of their road, and to deliver to the President and Directors of the Company, in payment of the subscription so made, bonds of the United States, payable at the will of the United States, and bearing interest at the rate of four per cent. per annum, payable semi-annually.

SEC. 2. *And be it further enacted,* That the Directors of such Railroad Companies, upon depositing four per cent. bonds of the United States with the Treasurer of the United States, to be held by him in trust, may and they are hereby authorized to establish a banking department, and to receive from the Comptroller of the Currency, bank notes of denominations not less than one dollar, nor more than one thousand dollars, for an amount equal to the par of the bonds so deposited, which notes shall be at the will of the holder converted into specie, or into national currency, or four per cent. convertible currency bonds of the United States, as the company issuing them may prefer. And such companies may, and they are hereby authorized, to carry on the business of banking, under such regulations as Congress may from time to time prescribe, and in case of failure to redeem their bank notes, upon demand, the holders may cause protest to be made, and should they not otherwise provide funds therefor, the Treasurer of the United States as trustee, upon thirty days notice of protest, shall redeem the same, and charge the sum thus paid, including the cost of protest, to the defaulting bank.

SEC. 3. *And be it further enacted*, That subscriptions payable thirty years after date, with interest at the rate of four per cent. per annum, payable in national currency, made by states, cities, towns, counties, and owners of land on the line of or near to the railroad, made under such regulations as the Legislature of the State may prescribe, and the payment of the interest on which shall be guaranteed by the State, in which the railroad is to be located, shall be accepted by the Supervisory Board, as satisfactory; and the company upon a deposit with the Treasurer of the United States, of four per cent. bonds of the United States, to be held by him as trustee for their redemption, may and is hereby authorized to receive from the Comptroller of the currency, a like sum in post notes of denominations not less than one dollar, payable in one, two, three, four or five years after date, with interest at a rate not exceeding four per cent. per annum, payable when the note becomes due, which notes shall at all times be receivable at par in payment for travel or transportation on their railroad, and in case of non payment when due, the holder may cause protest to be made, and if funds are not otherwise provided, upon thirty days notice of protest, the Treasurer as trustee, shall redeem the same, and charge the sum paid therefor, including the interest and cost of protest, to the defaulting bank. And in the case of the issue of post notes, the interest accruing on the bonds deposited, shall be invested by the Treasurer in the four per cent. bonds, and held in trust by him, as part of the fund pledged for the payment of the post notes issued as aforesaid.

Sec. 4. *And be it further enacted,* That the rate of interest charged by such companies upon discounts, shall not be more than four per cent. per annum, payable in advance, and that the rates charged for travel and transportation on their railroads, shall not be more than with the profits on the sum used in the banking department, will realize ten per cent. per annum, on the sums expended on the construction and equipment of their railroads, over and above their proper annual expenditures. And the dividends paid to shoreholders, shall at no time exceed four per cent. per annum, until the surplus earnings over and above four per cent. shall have created a sinking fund, equal to the cost of the construction and equipment of their railroads, and shall have created and placed a sum in the banking department to the credit of the subscribers respectively equal to their several subscriptions for the capital stock of said company; and when this shall have been done, the rates charged for travel and transportation on their railroads shall not be more than may be requisite to create a fund sufficient to pay the sum, which may be necessarily and properly expended in the management and repairs of their railroads. And the capital, business, and profits of the company, shall not be liable to any tax to be levied by authority of the United States, or of any State or Territory thereof.

Sec. 5. *And be it further enacted,* That the Supervisory Board may require such railroad company to make to them monthly reports, showing what their receipts and expenditures and what the management of their business and affairs has been.

The rates charged for the transportation of the mails and of the troops and munitions of the United States, shall be the same as may be charged for like service for others.

Sec. 6. *And be it further enacted,* That this act shall be in force from and after its passage.

Which was, after a lengthy discussion, referred to the Committee on Railroads Generally.

Mr. KENNARD, of Louisiana, by leave, offered the following:

WHEREAS, The demand for labor in this country exceeds the supply; and

WHEREAS, The true and long settled policy of this government, has been to offer every encouragement to voluntary immigration from all foreign countries, without distinction.

Be it resolved, By this Convention:

1. That only voluntary immigration is consistent with the true intents of the whole country.
2. That class legislation on this subject, is alike unwise and unwarranted by the Constitution of the United States.
3. That all foreign nations should enjoy the same rights of immigration to, and residence in every part of the United States.

Referred to Committee on Immigration

The Convention then adjourned to 8 o'clock, P. M.

EVENING SESSION.

The Convention assembled at 8 o'clock P. M., President GARRETT in the Chair.

Mr. MACCABE, of Arkansas, offered the following report of a Special Committee:

The Special Committee to whom was referred the resolution in reference to the war between France and Prussia, beg leave to report to the Convention the following preamble and resolution:

WHEREAS, The commercial relations of the United States with Europe, being seriously disturbed by the present calamitous war between France and Prussia; and

WHEREAS, The best interests of Europe and America are to be consulted in the establishment of permanent peace between the belligerents; therefore,

Resolved, That this Convention, representing the commercial interests of the whole country, respectfully but earnestly, request the President of the United States, to tender the good offices of the Government, for the restoration of permanent peace upon a basis consistent with the honor and dignity of the parties to the war.

Which was adopted.

Mr. MILLER, of Alabama, offered the following report of the Committee on Improvement of Seacoast, Lake and Gulf Harbors:

The Committee regret that information in detail, referring to the present condition and the necessities of the harbors on the Atlantic coast, has not been submitted to them from all the ports.

From such communications and statements as have been made, the Committee beg leave respectfully to report, that the harbors on the Southern Atlantic coast and rivers, with but few exceptions, are in such a condition as to materially impede the commerce of the country. These harbors have obstructions existing at their bars, and in their channel ways, of two distinct characters: 1st. There are obstructions existing from shifting sandbeds, under tidal influences, and 2d. Obstructions which have been placed in the principal channels, and which can be permanently removed.

These obstructions may be removed, by well directed efforts; but not without necessitating an outlay of money, to an amount which corporations reduced (in financial ability), as most of these ports have been, are unable to raise without imposing an oppressive taxation upon the inhabitants, already overburdened.

It is not, in the judgment of this Committee, deemed incumbent upon them to recommend any special plan for overcoming the harbor obstructions occasioned by shifting sand beds, or for removing such temporary obstructions as may have been placed in these great channel ways of commerce. We but refer to their existence, and with the sole object of directing the attention of the General Government to their removal at the earliest time possible. Large vessels have been sunk, and other obstructions of insignificant value but of incalculable damage, have been placed in the harbors of Richmond, Charleston and Savannah. Congress, when memorialized heretofore, has granted small appropriations for this purpose to the ports of Richmond and Charleston, but these have been wholly inadequate for the ends desired by these cities, while the harbor of Savannah has not received any appropriation whatever from the Government for the purposes heretofore indicated.

The port of Richmond, exporting merchandise on which the Government receives a revenue duty of $5,000,000 annually, has had but $50,000 appropriated for the removal of existing obstructions and for improving her harbor. The principal obstructions consist of a bar of sand and alluvium, on a rock base, a few miles below the city. It is the opinion of eminent engineers that when once properly removed the obstruction will no longer continue to exist, and in order to effect its accomplishment, and to give to the port the facilities it requires, it is recommended by this Committee that the sum of $250,000 be appropriated for the aforesaid purposes.

The port of Charleston, exporting a large amount of cotton, rice and lumber, and the principal entry port of the State of South Carolina, has received the trifling sum of $25,000, which has been barely enough to open a single inlet to the rich phosphate beds of this section, now becoming a considerable item of commercial traffic. The Committee recommend an appropriation of $300,000 for dredging this harbor and removing the obstructions existing in it of an artificial character.

The port of Savannah has, from its system of railway connection with the interior, become the third exporting point in rank on the whole Atlantic and Gulf coast of the United States. During the past season 1869-70, there has been shipped from this port 506,840 bales of cotton, besides a large amount of rice, lumber and naval stores, aggregating the value of these exports at the sum of near 70,000,000. Congress has failed to grant an appropriation of any sum to Savannah for the improvements of her harbor, which this Committee would beg leave to respectfully urge at this time. The momentum of the current of the Savannah river is such that it is thought that if a proper appropriation be granted the difficulties now existing may be permanently overcome, and this Committee recommend that the sum of $400,000 be appropriated by the General Government for removing all obstructions placed in the Savannah river at or near the city, and for the improvement of this harbor.

The stimulus given to the trade in fruits and the products peculiar to the climate of Florida, make it necessary, in the opinion of this Committee, that the General Government should grant an appropriation to open the channel of the lower St. John's river at and below Jacksonville, and to this end we recommend to the General Government an appropriation of $200,000.

The Committee having had submitted to them the subject of harbors for refuge on our Northern lakes, would respectfully recommend to the General Government the continued appropriations for the establishment of these harbors at such points as have been designated by the United States Corps of Engineers, especially Michigan city, Indiana, Chicago and Calumet river, Illinois, Milwaukee, Wisconsin, and such other points on Lake Michigan, Superior, Huron, Erie and Ontario, as have already been recommended as essential to the protection of the large and increasing commerce of these lakes.

The Committee are indebted to Collector THOMAS P. ROBB, of Savannah, for a valuable statistical report which is hereto appended, and which they ask shall be taken as a part of this report.

In reporting upon Gulf coast harbors, your Committee would, out of deference to the Committee assigned the special duty of reporting upon the Mississippi river's harbor and bar, remit to that committee the labors respecting that most momentous interest, but can not resist the temptation to say, that the prodigious commerce of this river makes its improvement national, and the legitimate charge of the General Government to the amount of whatever thousands or millions it may cost to give it deep channels to sea, and entire safety of transit to that commerce.

ATCHAFALAYA.

The first channel west of the Mississippi demanding the attention of the Government is the Atchafalaya bay and channel.

About 100 miles west of the mouths of the Mississippi, this bay receives the extravasated waters of Red river, and of the Mississippi above their confluence, and below that confluence to the Plaquemine bayou. It has a commerce and interior navigation in its connection of vast importance. It has a bar of only 7 feet of water from the gulf into the bay, and thence, with a tortuous channel through the bay of about 10 feet for 18 miles to the mouth of the Atchafalaya river, enters a deep channel and harbor of indefinite extent. This channel through the bay is now being dredged and straightened by the enterprise and purse of a single individual, whose line of steamships thence to the Texas coast have made about 400 trips across the bars per year.

As this channel is destined to be the outlet of all the trade from the Mississippi to the coast of Louisiana, Texas, Mexico and Central America, by a route some 300 miles shorter than by the mouths of the Mississippi, we believe that it most urgently demands an appropriation from the national treasury for deepening the channel across the bar to the depth of the bay channel, and the straightening and clearing out of the bay channel itself. Both works are comparatively light, and the nature of their bottom such as to promise permanence after their completion.

SABINE PASS AND HARBORS.

The Sabine river has about 800 miles of interior navigation, and is the natural outlet of the productions of west Louisiana and eastern Texas. Upon its waters and tributary to it as an outlet, lie some 5000 square miles of the best pine and white oak forests in America. The bar at its mouth is not wide or difficult of deepening from its present depth, of 8 feet, to admit vessels of 12 feet, the average depth of lake Sabine, through which the river flows.

We believe this improvement to be properly the work of the General Government, and recommend that a survey be made, and adequate appropriations for its improvement.

The Committee would here remark, that the bar at this rivers' mouth, is like that of the Mississippi river; and hence, that treatment which may be found best for the mouths of that great river, will be adapted to the bar of the Sabine.

GALVESTON BAY, BAR, AND HARBORS.

At a distance of 60 miles south-west of the Sabine, lies Galveston bay, with its double harbors, and inner and outer bars. The channel over the outer bar to Galveston bay, has 13 feet water, admitting vessels of 12 feet draft at mean tide. It has maintained this depth during the historic period, and this may be assumed as its natural regimen. The bar at the mouth of the Galveston harbor, into the pass, has but 9 feet water at the present time; and the tendencies of nature are manifestly to close the mouth of this harbor, unless a proper remedy be early applied.

The harbor of Galveston has 20 to 27 feet of water, and the entire pass, known both as Bolivar pass and Galveston pass, has 20 to 40 feet water to the outer bar; and hence, any work by which these two bars shall be cut to the depth of 15 or 20 feet, will be efficient in giving a navigation for the largest vessels into Bolivar (Galveston) pass, and up to the wharves in front of the city of Galveston.

When we reflect that Galveston bay is the only inlet for more than 8 feet water, for 1,000 miles of coast, West of the Mississippi; that this bay represents the seafront and main outlet for the commerce of the great trans-Mississippi, with some arid area of 500 miles from East to West, and of near 1,400 miles from North to South, that already it is the harbor of nearly 100,000,000 of commerce, in and outward bound; and that when her railroads, now far progressed, shall connect across the Indian Territories to the

States of the North-west, that commerce will be doubled and quadrupled in a few years; we are strongly fortified in our claim upon the General Government, for such early and substantial aid in its rescue from impending loss, and its enlargement and deepening to an extent proportioned to its present and prospective servitudes.

BRAZOS RIVER.

The Brazos river, represents about 100 miles of river navigation, and connects with canal navigation, and interior coast line navigation of indefinite extent, present and prospective. The bar at the mouth of the Brazos river, generally known as a sand bar, is, however, chiefly composed of clayey dsposits from that river, and is covered usually with a crust of gulf sand. It has a variable depth of 5 to 12 feet water, rarely being reliable for vessels of more than 8 feet draft.

But for this fluctuating bar the city of the Texas coast would have been built at Valasco, on the main land, instead of its present site, upon Galveston island, for the channel of the river inside has a depth of 20 to 40 feet, and a width of about 600 feet for 40 miles up, to Columbia, presenting such security of harbor in all its lengths as is unknown to any harbor West of the Mississippi.

We commend it to the attention of the Government for the solution of the very doubtful question of its improvement.

PASS CAVALLO.

At 80 miles South-west from the Brazos river, is the pass Cavallo, with a somewhat changeable bar of 8 feet water, entering to the Matagorda and Lavaca bays. Could this bar be kept at 12 feet water, which, it is believed, would be practicable, that depth could be carried up to Saluria, and thence, by dredging, to Indianola. Lavaca bay, however, has an average depth of about 9 feet—say 8 feet for navigation—with sundry bars, recently cut to this depth by the enterprise of the Lavaca Dredging and Canal Company. Nothing that we can properly denominate as a harbor exists, however, at either of the sites named; but as the waters are not very deep, a harbor proper is less demanded.

We commend to the Government of the United States the improvement of this bar, as representing a vast trade from interior Texas, both by interior navigation of bays and inlets, and by the rail system now developing toward Austin and San Antonio.

ARANSAS AND CORPUS CHRISTI BARS AND HARBORS.

Proceeding down the gulf coast a distance of 60 miles, we find Aransas pass and harbor, with a variable bar of 8 to 12 feet water. The importance of this pass can not be overrated. It opens to the Aransas bay with 20 to 40 feet depth of water, into St. Joseph harbor, only 1½ miles from the bar, and thence, with 9 feet water, up to the main land at Rockport, and other points along the Aransas bay, and in like manner it opens with like depth to Corpus Christi bay, the passes to which bay have recently been dredged by the great enterprise of the Corpus Christi Ship Canal Company, to carry the same depth through the bay of 12 to 18 feet up to that city.

When we bear in mind that this is the most Westerly point of navigation on the gulf, and that from this point the Mexican trade, as well as that of South-western Texas, has always found, and must forever in the future find, its outlet to the sea; that here Gen. Taylor, with the armies of the United States, debarked on his route to the conquest of interior Mexico. These considerations, the Committee believe, justify us in claiming for the Aransas bar, such surveys and improvements as the magnitude of the interests thus involved would indicate and warrant.

The most important point on the gulf of Mexico that requires attention after New Orleans, is the port of Mobile. Before the war, its exports exceeded a half million of bales of cotton, in addition to large quantities of lumber, staves and other products of the forest. Since the war, its exports have been less, but still they exceed 300,000 bales of cotton, and embrace large shipments of lumber. Its direct foreign imports are considerable, while its imports from domestic ports, corresponds to the amount of its exports. It is the natural outlet of the sections of country watered by the Alabama, Bigbee and Warrior rivers, and is the natural market of South Alabama, East Mississippi, and a portion of Georgia.

Mobile is connected by rail with the Western States, by means of the Mobile & Ohio Railroad, which extends 472 miles to the mouth of the Ohio, and with New Orleans, Memphis, Pensacola and Montgomery, and by means of connecting roads, with Louisville, Vicksburg and the whole railroad system of the South, North and West.

There is also a direct water communication between Mobile and New Orleans, which is protected from the storms and winds of the gulf, by a chain of islands extending from the mouth of the bay to lakes Pontchartrain and Borgne, in Louisiana. Owing to the difficulties experienced at the mouth of the Mississippi, direct water communication is about being opened between that river, and the waters of lake Borgne, whereby vessels from the Western cities can pass without interruption, from the Mississippi into the waters of Mobile bay.

This bay offers anchorage to vessels of the largest class; its outer bar permits the entrance of vessels of 24 feet draft. This anchorage is of sufficient size to accommodate hundreds of vessels; it is safe, being entirely land-locked, and protected from the winds and waves of the gulf, with holding ground not excelled by that of any other harbor.

This place of anchorage, is but a few miles from the track of vessels from Brazil and South America—even when destined to Northern ports, and which naturally seek the advantage of the gulf stream to aid them on their voyage. This fact in connection with the short distance at which this harbor lies from the West Indies, indicates it as the most advantageous point to which the West Indian and South American commerce of the valley of the Mississippi can be directed. Its value is still further increased by the consideration that by the rail facilities it possesses, this harbor can be utilized to the Great West, in less time, and at less expense, than any other port in the country.

To enable the nation to obtain the full advantage of this port of the gulf, all that is needed is the deepening of the natural channels between this anchorage and the city of Mobile. A depth of 18 feet water exists to within 20 miles of the city; thence the water gradually and slowly shoals to 15 feet, and then 13 feet, till the Dog river bar is reached, at the distance of about 9 to 10 miles below the city. At this point, partly from the deposits produced by that small stream, which enters the bay from the West, and partly from the effect of artificial obstructions placed there during the late war, the depth is reduced to about 9 feet. This shallow water exists for the span of a few hundred yards, and the water deepens again after passing this bar, and with the exception of a small span in what is known as Choctaw pass, 15 feet water can be carried to the city.

Surveys of the harbor and of these channels have been carefully made, and no doubt is entertained by the engineers who have examined the localities, that these shallows are capable of being permanently removed, and a sufficient depth of water permanently maintained.

The citizens of the city and county of Mobile, have been willing to tax themselves, to deepen these channels, and laws for that purpose have been obtained. At its last session, Congress made a small appropriation of $50,000 towards this work, which is now being applied under the direction of its engineer officers. This amount will be of service, and will be used to open the Choctaw pass, to a depth sufficient to allow vessels, which can pass Dog river bar, to come to the city by that channel, instead of being compelled to use the longer routes by way of Spanish river.

This sum, however, is entirely inadequate to effect the desired improvement.

The U. S. Engineer, to whom the work was confided, reports that it is entirely feasible to remove the obstructions at Dog river, and to secure a channel of 13 feet depth, with a width of 300 feet, which shall be permanent, at an expenditure of $716,000. To secure 15 feet, would require an additional outlay of $500,000.

If a less width of channel be accepted, a proportionate increase of depth can be obtained in the same outlay of money, so that probably a depth of 15 to 17 feet, with a width of 200 feet can be secured, at an outlay of $1,000,000.

Your Committee, in view of these facts, which seem to be clearly established as to the feasibility of the work, and of its great importance for commercial purposes, which a mere inspection of the map will establish, to say nothing of its vast importance for military purposes in case of war, with any considerable maritime power, recommend that the Convention present to Congress the improvement of the bay and harbor of Mobile, by deepening its navigable channels to a depth sufficient to accommodate vessels to the city wharves of at least 15 feet, as a work of great national importance, and which should be done at national expense.

The Committee also recommend that the harbor at Ship island and Mississippi city, which lies at about midway between the cities of Mobile and New Orleans, be commended to the attention of Congress for improvement.

This locality is about to be brought into prominence by the canal now in progress of construction between the Mississippi river and Lake Borgne, and which will vastly aid the commerce of the gulf and the valley of the Mississippi, and tend to furnish some relief from the difficulties to that commerce by reason of the bar at the mouth of that river, which so far have proved so unmanageable.

The Committee recommend the adoption of the following resolution:

Resolved, That the Secretary of this Convention furnish to the members of Congress from the States represented in this Convention a copy of the foregoing report and this resolution, with the request that they present the same to Congress at its next session, and use all their influence to obtain the necessary appropriations to secure the improvement of the harbors herein recommended.

The report, after a lengthy discussion, was unanimously adopted.

Mr. HASTIE, of South Carolina, by unanimous leave, offered the following:

WHEREAS, The causes which led to the late unfortunate contest between the different sections of these United States has ceased to exist, and the Government of the United States being established upon a firm and solid basis, with a strength and power, financially and physically, equal to any government in the world; it becomes that Government, in the plenitude of its power, to pass a bill of general amnesty, which in its effect "will be a blessing to those who grant, as well as to those who receive;" effectually healing those wounds which have been partially effaced by commercial association; therefore,

Resolved, That a committee of three members of this Convention be appointed by the Chair, to petition the Congress of the United States, in behalf of this Convention, to pass a bill of general amnesty.

After a protracted and general discussion, Mr. GIBBONS, of Pennsylvania, offered the following amendment:

Resolved, That the Southern Commercial Convention of 1870 pass, by a vote of acclamation, a request that the Congress of the United States pass a bill for the repeal of all test oaths, and the removal of all political disabilities on American citizens.

After some discussion of this resolution, Mr. CHEEVER, of Michigan, offered the following as a second amendment:

Resolved, That in the deliberations of this Convention we have known no North, no South, no East, no West. We have met to deliberate as American citizens, and as such we will hail with pleasure the time when all political disabilities shall be removed by the Government.

Mr. CORWINE, of Ohio, offered as a substitute for the whole, the following:

Resolved, That the delegates of this Convention unanimously request Congress to pass a law granting general amnesty to the people of the South, and the repeal of all laws requiring test oaths, so as remove all political disabilities wherever they exist.

The question being taken on Mr. CORWINE's substitute, the Chair announced that the vote was unanimously, heartily and cordially in the affirmative.

This announcement was received with prolonged and general applause.

On motion of Mr. BRYSON, of Missouri, the Convention adjourned until 9 o'clock, A. M., of Friday, Oct. 7, 1870.

FOURTH DAY.

The Convention assembled at 9.50 o'clock A. M., Hon. JOHN W. GARRETT, presiding.

The proceedings were opened by prayer by M. C. T. BRIGGS, of Trinity Church, Cincinnati.

Mr. LILLY, of Virginia, offered the following:

WHEREAS, There are many meritorious young men in our country struggling to obtain a collegiate education, notwithstanding their limited means, and the professors of the colleges have shown great liberality in such cases; and

WHEREAS, The expense of traveling from some portions of the country to those where institutions of learning are furnished with all the appliances for imparting thorough instruction and the best educational advantages are enjoyed, is a serious obstacle in the way of many of these young men in acquiring the education they wish; therefore,

Resolved, That a committee of three be appointed by the President of this Convention to ascertain from the authorities of the several railroads whether they will be willing to pass such students of colleges over their roads at half their usual rates of fare. The committee to report to the next Commercial Convention.

Which was, on motion of Mr. REMELIN, of Ohio, laid on the table.

Mr. BOWMAN, of Kentucky, by unanimous consent, offered the following:

Resolved, That a committee of five be appointed by the Chair, to be called the Committee on Education, whose duty it shall be to submit to the next meeting of this Convention a report upon the subject of education as related to the commercial and industrial interests of the country, and as adapted especially to the wants of the masses of the South and West.

Which was unanimously adopted.

Gen. BANKS, of Massachusetts, in accordance with instructions of Committee on Southern Pacific Railway, offered the following:

Resolved, That the President of the Convention be requested to appoint a committee representing the section of the country especially interested in the construction of the Southern Pacific Railway, and present, for the consideration of the President and Congress of the United States, the views of the Convention and its deep interest in the success of this important national enterprise.

Resolved, That the officers of the Convention be directed to transmit to the President of the United States, the President of the Senate and Speaker of the House of Representatives, a certified copy of the foregoing resolution.

Which were adopted.

Mr. BISHOP, of Ohio, presented a communication from C. W. ROWLAND, President of Cincinnati Chamber of Commerce, inviting the members of the Convention to attend on 'Change at 12.30 o'clock P. M., 7th inst., to listen to an address by Hon. N. P. BANKS.

The invitation was accepted by a unanimous vote of the Convention.

Mr. BURWELL, of Louisiana, offered the following, which was adopted.

Resolved, That the city of New Orleans, the outlet port of the Mississippi valley, and other gulf ports of the United States, are entitled to, and should receive at the hands of the Government, the same or similar subventions for postal steam service to foreign ports as has been or shall be bestowed upon the Atlantic ports of the United States.

Mr. ELLIOTT, of Missouri, offered the following:

Resolved, That this Convention respectfully represents to the Congress of the United States, that the public interests would be greatly subserved by a liberal grant of lands to secure the construction of a branch Pacific Railway, leaving the line of the Kansas Pacific Railway at some point not east of the 97th meridian of longitude, and striking the line of the Atlantic & Pacific Railway at some point east of Albuquerque in New Mexico. That such branch railway would prove of great use to the Government in military and postal service, would accommodate a large commerce of New Mexico, Arizona, and Chihuahua, would afford additional facilities in developing the mineral and other resources of the interior mountain regions, and would greatly aid in redeeming the western portion of the great plains to civilized uses.

Which was referred to the Committee on Trans latitudinal Railways.

Mr. BRYSON, of Missouri, presented and read the report of the Committee on the Construction of Permanent Levees on the Mississippi river, as follows:

In entering upon the discussion of this subject, your Committee beg leave first to present a statement of the extent and nature of the region sought to be reclaimed.

It embraces all the alluvian liable to overflow by the Mississippi river, from the bluffs near Cape Girardeau, in Missouri, on its West bank, and near Memphis, Tennessee, on its East bank, and a point 45 miles below New Orleans, in the State of Louisiana, and is estimated by Generals Humphreys and Abbot, in their elaborate survey, to contain about 21,000,000 acres of the richest land in the world.

The value of this land, however, is not so much on account of the fertility of its soil, as the nature of its products—cotton and sugar—both articles of prime necessity, and second to none in commercial importance.

The cotton supply is a problem engaging the attention of the civilized world, and to be able to furnish the needed supply, and so gain a great commercial victory, has been taxing the inginuity and energies of the leading commercial nations of the globe.

England has not only given encouragement to Egypt, Turkey, Brazil, Peru, Morrocco and Japan, in the production of this staple, but has actually loaned her credit to the amount of $460,000,000, to develop the cotton production in India, and is willing to double the sum.

The time was when the United States held the monopoly of the cotton supply.

In 1860, she produced 5,196,444, in 1869, she produced about 3,000,000 bales. Can she afford to lose this great commercial advantage? We answer, most decidedly. No! If ever there was a time she required this advantage, it is now.

The Special Commissioner of Revenue, in his report to the recent session of Congress, makes the following startling statement: that we increased our foreign indebtedness during the previous year, by the enormous sum of $210,000,000. $80,000,000 of this was to pay interest on debt previously held there.

That we have not felt the shock of this movement, is because we have a convenient medium with which to meet this, viz: Government bonds. However, we must remember, that although they appear as values exported, that they are not real values, but only deferred payment, or promises to pay.

Let us continue a few years longer this operation, exporting bonds to pay interest on bonds, increasing the amount by compounding, and we ask any reasonable man what will be the result. When in exporting bonds to pay interest on bonds we have shipped the last bond, which at the present rate will be in less than ten years, the next draft will be on our specie, and bankruptcy and ruin must ensue. We repeat it, we can not afford to continue this ruinous process. It is commercial suicide. The remedy lies within our grasp. We can and must assert our old supremacy in the supply of cotton. With an efficient system of levees we need fear no competitor. In these rich alluvial lands, a greatly superior staple can be produced, at half the cost of production in India, and in a few years, 7,000,000 acres could be prepared and set apart for its cultivation, leaving ample space for all other productions essential to the planting interest, and yielding annually, from 7,000,000 to 10,000,000 bales of cotton.

In the face of such an opportunity, it is certainly the hight of national imbecility, nay more, it is a crime to leave those splendid acres to the mercy of the floods; and it is doubly so, when we consider the sugar supply.

During the fiscal year ending June 30, 1870, the value of sugars imported for consumption, reached the enormous amount of $67,-000,000, while with an efficient system of levees, over 4,000,000 acres can be set apart for its production, yielding double the quantity required for our most extravagant consumption. Even prior to the war, with mere patch-work of levees, we were enabled to produce nearly three times the quantity produced in 1863.

We repeat it, it can not be short of a national crime to ignore such opportunities.

By the foregoing facts which are undoubtedly true, and can easily be verified by any one who will take the pains, it is evident that in reclaiming these lands by an efficient system of levees, the amount of our imports will be reduced in the article of sugar, about $70,000,000, and our exportation of cotton increased by a greater amount, thus providing annually not less than $150,000,000 to pay off our foreign indebtedness.

Waiving then the further discussion of the great value of these lands and the national and commercial advantages of their reclamation, we turn to the questions: Is their reclamation possible? and how is it to be done?

The possibility of constructing and maintaining such a system of levees as will ensure protection will not admit of a doubt. On this point we quote the statement of Senators HUMPHREYS and ABBOT, in their report to Congress made in 1866, and repeated in their report of 1869. They say:

"The levees contemplated in these estimates are large, much larger than residents of the alluvial lands in general anticipate, but would not, when greatest, exceed in magnitude those on the right branch of the Rhine, below Arnheim, which protect the most fertile part of Holland. These levees are exposed at high water to as strong a current as that of the Mississippi in flood, and also to the destructive effects of ice. But the occurrence of crevasses such as take place with every great flood of the Mississippi, are there unknown. The supervision, watching and care of these levees is costly, but effective and remunerative. While the levees of the Mississippi are trifling compared to the interests they protect."

The construction and proper policing of such a system of levees as are recommended by Senators HUMPHREY and ABBOT would without doubt afford absolute security from overflow. This brings us to the important practical question:

HOW CAN THIS BE SECURED?

That we have never possessed such a system the history of the past fully demonstrates. Even immediately previous to the war, which destroyed such as we had, when the system was in its most perfect condition, the two distinguished named engineers speak of them as follows:

"As they stand throughout the greater part of the valley, they encourage delusive hopes of protection. Whenever the river rises three feet above its natural banks, diasastrous crevasses are sure to occur, and if every break upon the river were now closed, any flood worthy of the name would be sure to open new ones of sufficient numbers to devastate large areas of the alluvial lands."

The system here spoken of was at best but a patchwork of levees. They were constructed and maintained under the supervision of the States, counties, parishes, or even smaller levee districts, each separate authority having its own special plan, and governing itself accordingly. We believe such varied authority can never secure a uniform and intelligent system. The Committee would therefore report and recommend the adoption of the following:

WHEREAS, The reclamation from overflow of the alluvial land lying upon the Mississippi river and its tributaries, in the States of Louisiana, Arkansas, Mississippi, Tennessee and Missouri, is a work of the first importance to the entire nation, and will greatly increase the public wealth and establish the national credit; and

WHEREAS, The experience of the past demonstrates that this can not be accomplished through separate State action.

Be it resolved, by this Convention, That national aid should be promptly and liberally afforded to this enterprise, and such laws enacted by Congress consistent with the rights of the States as will place the whole Mississippi levee system under one control.

After a lengthy discussion, the report and accompanying resolution were adopted.

Mr. EMLEY, of Louisiana, presented the following resolution as the report of the Committee on Railway Viaducts over Navigable Rivers:

Resolved, That this Convention deems it highly important that all railway bridges over navigable rivers be made highways for railroads, and that legislation to that effect is hereby recommended, with suitable provision for an equitable apportionment of the cost of construction and maintenance of such bridges, amongst the railroad companies using the same.

Which was adopted.

Mr. WILLIAMSON, of Tennessee, presented and read the following report of the Committee on Continuous Water Line Communication between the Mississippi River and the Atlantic Seaboard, as follows:

The Committee to which was assigned the duty of reporting upon a Continuous Water Line Communication between the Mississippi River and the Atlantic Seaboard, and along the Western Gulf Coast, would beg leave to report:

That the various papers referred to them and the reports of standing committees have been duly considered, and are embodied in the following report:

First. They would call special attention of this Convention to the able paper drawn up by Mr. Monroe, of Iowa, chairman of the committee charged with the duty of memorializing Congress upon this subject, at the last meeting of this Convention; and the Committee beg to make his paper a portion of this report.

Second. The Committee then would add the able paper of Col. Raiford, of Florida, upon the coast line east of the Mississippi, and across the State of Florida, together with the report thereon by the Jacksonville, Florida, Board of Trade, and beg to make them a portion of this report.

Third. The Committee further add the elaborate report of Col. Forshey, upon the line west of the Mississippi and south to the Rio Grande.

CONTINUOUS INLAND WATER LINE COMMUNICATION WEST FROM THE MISSISSIPPI RIVER ALONG THE GULF COAST TO RIO GRANDE. BY COL. FORSHEY, OF TEXAS.

In the slow encroachments of the land upon the gulf of Mexico, along its western margin, as upon the east, by washings from the land, and by the retiring of the sea, or perhaps by the very gradual uprising of the entire gulf coast line, there have been left, as if by some beneficent disposition in favor of human want and human industry, a series of lakes, lagoons, shallow bays and inland channels, connecting or nearing them, that leave but little effort by the hand of man to unite them all by short canal cuts, in such manner as to give us continuous inland navigation nearly parallel to the gulf along its entire coast.

A glance at the map of western Louisiana will show something of this disposition of the waters; and yet, only a very small part of these channels adapted to commercial uses have found their way into any map, and are known only to the local explorers, surveyors and engineers, and the semi-aquatic fishermen and oystermen that live in boats among these channels.

Commencing five miles above New Orleans, we find the Canal de la Compagnie, connecting by a lock with the Mississippi, and passing boats thence by a cut and old bayou channel, about six miles, into Lake Catouatchie; and passing thence through this and Lake Washa, by a cut through the marsh and trembling prairie, to the Lafourche, at Lockport, about 40 miles from the river. It continues across the Lafourche to Lake Fields, and by a short cut to Lake Long, and to the Bayou Terre Bonne. The navigation of this canal, by suitable increase of width, would be easy and safe for steamboats; and by very little work, the Terre Bonne to the Bayou Black, and that bayou to Berwick's bay, 90 miles by this water line from New Orleans, would be easy and always safe.

From the Atchafalaya, below the Berwick's bay proper, there is good and deep bayou connection, through nameless channels in the marsh, as there is always safe navigation by way of Atchafalaya bay into Cote Blanche bay, and through this, into Vermilion bay. This bay has, like Atchafalaya and Cote Blanche, some 6 feet depth of water, and its western projection reaches 75 miles west of Berwick's bay.

From Vermilion into Flat lake and Pecan lake, a cut of 2 miles in the marsh would give 20 more miles of channel.

From Pecan into Lake Mermentau, the distance of some 10 miles would have to be cut with like level mud marsh for banks.

Mermentau lake and river (always navigable, and in constant use from the sea) would give us 20 miles more of navigation.

From the Mermentau river through Lake Calcasieu to Sabine lake, a distance of some 30 miles, the connections are not well known to the reporter, but it is likely that half the distance of 30 miles would have to be cut through a similar salt marsh.

We here reach Lake Sabine, on the boundary of Texas and Louisiana, by an inland series of channels already existing, except about 27 miles to be cut, the total distance being about 250 miles.

INLAND COAST NAVIGATION IN TEXAS.

Texas has a coast line front of 400 miles, not including indentations, which would swell it to more than 600 miles. In this whole distance the line of interior bays and channels; only narrowly separated from the gulf, extends almost continuously.

From Sabine bay Taylor's bayou furnishes a channel westward to within 10 miles of Elm and East bayous, which pass into East Galveston bay. These bayous would require widening and deepening in places. The cut between them would be through level prairie with clay bottom, and without rocks or obstacles; 10 miles of canal would connect navigation, and give 60 miles navigation. Thence, the Galveston and West bays, and the canal already in use, give us 46 miles to the Brazos river. Thence to the Cancy creek, the cut through the level prairies and very shallow lagoons would be about 20 miles, one-fourth of which would be supplied by partial or natural channels.

The Caney is connected with Matagorda bay by a short canal of half a mile; and thence the Matagorda bay furnishes our route with channel and safe navigation for 62 miles to Saluria. Here Pass Cavallo connects with the gulf, the second pass of importance in Texas.

From Saluria, the channel is open and in use, with a few cuts through Oyster reefs through Espiritu Santo, San Antonio, Aransas, and Corpus Christi bays, a distance of about 85 miles; this route crossing the Aransas pass at 65 miles, a channel in constant use for both government supplies and the purposes of general commerce.

From Corpus Christi bay our water line down the Laguna Madre is unbroken to the Rio Grande, 125 miles, this channel has never been navigated because of many shoal sand bars that traverse it, and which would require to be dredged. Nothing but sand, shells and clay, however, would be found to obstruct dredging.

Thus the ent're inland coast navigation in Texas would be nearly 400 miles, of which distance the canal cutting would not exceed 30 miles.

In consideration then, of the grand dispositions of Nature in our favor, in presenting us channels for inland navigation from the Mississippi to the Rio Grande, some 650 miles of distance, if we will but connect the links by about 55 miles of canal, at a cost of not more than $30,000 per mile; and of a like distance in the opposite direction to the Atlantic across the Florida peninsula, about 650 miles, with fragmentary canals of about 120 miles.

And in consideration of the vast inland navigation with which this work would connect the trade of the Mississippi valley, from which it is now cut off, amounting to about 3,500 miles east of the Mississippi, and about 3,500 miles west of river.

And in consideration of the fact that the commerce, the productions of that river and its tributaries, do actually reach a portion of these regions by most expensive land routes, and that a large portion of these districts are not customers of this valley for want of these lines of communication:

The Committee would recommend to the Convention the following resolutions:

Resolved, That a committee of three be appointed by the President of this Convention, charged with the duty of prosecuting this investigation and inquiry, to call upon the various Boards of Trade and Chambers of Commerce, and steamboat and mercantile, manufacturing and producing interests, for substantial aid in prosecuting the reconnoissance and surveys; and that they report the maps, plans, estimates and statistics of this great interest to the next meeting of this Convention.

Resolved, That in view of the obstructions to continuous navigation of Red river, through a distance of 2,000 miles, by the raft of some 40 miles near Shreveport in Louisiana, midway on the navigable channel of this river; and in view of the fact that this navigation relates to four States and Territories, and is not the special charge of either, at the same time that it represents a vast commerce; that we do most urgently pray the United States Congress to make liberal appropriations for the opening the channel to an extent demanded by its great importance to navigation.

Resolved, That the thanks of this Convention are due to Col. RAIFORD, a citizen of Texas, but recently occupied in Florida, for the unselfish energy with which he has explored the portion of the route east of the Mississippi river, and that he be requested to serve upon that committee.

The report and resolutions, under a call for the previous question, were adopted.

Mr. WILLIAMSON also presented the following from the same Committee:

While the people of the West have regarded the subject of cheap and safe transportation between the commercial centers of that section and the gathering points of foreign and domestic trade on the Atlantic seaboard as paramount to all others; and while commercial and internal improvement conventions have adopted resolutions and memorials relative to proposed water ways to cheapen the carrying trade between the Mississippi valley and the Atlantic ocean, one of the most feasible and economical routes for such a work has, so far, been overlooked.

When the canal now being constructed from the Mississippi river to Lake Borgne is completed, inland navigation will be established from that river to the eastern or Bon Secour arm of Mobile bay—168 miles—in a direct line to the nearest point on the Atlantic coast. Proceeding eastward from the Mississippi river, the first and perhaps the most important link in this chain of coast-line communication is already nearly formed by the Lake Borgne canal, to be completed in the course of the next six months. The Lake Borgne canal ten miles below New Orleans will connect the Mississippi with Lake Borgne and Mississippi sound by means of a reliable water communication, navigable not only by the steamboats and barges navigating the Mississippi, but also by sailing vessels in the coast trade, thus connecting the 16,700 miles of the navigable waters of the Mississippi and its tributaries with the 5,000 additional miles afforded by the Proel, Pascagoula, Alabama and Tombigbee rivers, together with their several tributaries. This important canal communication will not only enable the steamboats and barges loading at Cincinnati and other points in the Mississippi valley to unload at Mobile, Selma and Montgomery, but, what is of equal importance, bring the great West in direct water communication with Ship Island harbor, one of the best harbors on the gulf coast and only about 60 miles from New Orleans, while the South-west pass is 130 miles from that city, thus saving some 70 miles in distance, and obviating altogether the obstructions at the mouth of the Mississippi river. There is no good reason why the grain and other products of the Mississippi valley should not be reshipped upon deep draft vessels in Ship Island harbor.

The Lake Borgne canal will complete the coast line connection from the Mississippi river to Bon Secours bay, on the eastern side of Mobile bay, a distance of 168 miles.

The following is the report of Col. P. H RAIFORD, of Florida before referred to, which the Committee had adopted as a part of their report, and would respectfully recommend its adoption by the Convention:

While the people of the West have regarded the subject of cheap and safe transportation between the commercial centers of that section and the gathering points of foreign and domestic trade on the Atlantic seaboard as paramount to all others; and while commercial and internal improvement conventions have adopted resolutions and memorials relative to proposed water ways to cheapen the carrying trade between the Mississippi valley and the Atlantic ocean, the most feasible and economical route for such a work has, so far, been overlooked. The canal now being cut to connect by an inland passage the Mississippi river with the harbors of Mississippi sound and Mobile bay, will establish inland navigation to the eastern or Bon Secour arm of Mobile bay—168 miles—in a direct line to the nearest point on the Atlantic coast. From Mobile bay to the bay of St. Marks, Florida, the distance is 220 miles. Between these points, in almost a continuous line, parallel with the gulf shore, there is a succession of land-locked sounds, bays, lakes and lagoons, which, in the aggregate, make a navigable water way 160 miles in length. These sheets of water are Perdido and Pensacola bays, Santa Rosa sound, and the bays of Chactahatchee and St. Andrew's, Scearcey's river and lake Winuco, Apalachicola bay, St. George's sound, Crooked river, Oklockonee and Shallow bays, and other smaller inlets and lagoons along the gulf shore to the bay of St. Marks. Thus, it will be seen, that for a distance of 330 miles, from the proposed Mississippi and Pontchartrain canal to the bay of St. Marks, the canaling necessary to be done to create inland navigation to the latter point, does not exceed 60 miles in length, and all of which would be through the intervening strips of low ground and salt marsh but a few feet above the level of the sea. From the bay of St. Marks, following the gulf shore, and crossing the mouth of the three small rivers, Oceilla, Econfenco, and Finchollee, to the mouth of Little Warrior river, the distance is about 35 miles, the ground low and marshy, and susceptible of easy and cheap opening. From the mouth of the Warrior river—due east—to the confluence of the Suwanee and Santa Fe rivers, the distance is 45 miles—the land low and level, nowhere exceeding 30 feet above the level of the gulf.

From the Mississippi river to the latter point—the confluence of the Suwanee and Santa Fe rivers—450 miles, and within 60 miles of deep tide waters of the St. John's river of East Florida, a canal of any required dimensions may be made by the simplest character of work—mere ditching—to connect the inlets bordering the coasts of the gulf of Mexico, and a cut through the flat palmetto section between the Warrior and Suwanee rivers. From thence, through the short valleys of Santa Fe and Black creek—a deep tributary of the St. John's—which streams, flowing in opposite directions, have interlocked sources on a narrow dividing ridge where no engineering difficulties whatever would be found to prevent the continuation of this proposed water way, so as to create uninterrupted steamboat navigation between the Mississippi river and the capacious Atlantic harbors of Fernandina, Brunswick, Savannah, Port Royal and Charleston.

Counting the lengths of the gulf coast inlets, and those portions of the Santa Fe river and Black creek that can by improvement be made available, the actual canaling and dredging necessary to establish a continuous navigable water line, of uniform tide level, from Lake Borgne to the Atlantic ocean would not be more thañ 120 miles.

The most exposed portion of this gulf shore route, to the influence of the swells of the ocean, is along the Mississippi sound from Biloxi to Grant's pass, at the entrance of Mobile bay; yet, for many years, this sound has been navigated by ordinary, high-decked, river steamers, plying with heavy cargoes between interior towns on the Alabama and Tombigbee rivers and New Orleans, by way of the new canal, with as much safety and at the same rates of insurance as upon the Mississippi or Alabama rivers.

A reference to the map accompanying the United States coast survey reports will show the depth of water in the chain of inlets along the gulf shore, as well as the necks of land which would have to be cut through, for proper navigable connections, and which, when once made, would be kept free and open by the ebb and flow of the tides, secure from injury from either the storm of the gulf, or from river floods.

Such an improvement, of more value to the West and South, than any other projected, if made as it can be, of sufficient breadth and depth to permit the easy and quick passage of steamers engaged in the Western trade, would place the heavy and bulky commodities of the Mississippi valley in cheaper access to the great thoroughfares of commercial exchange, foreign and domestic, than can be done by any other means whatever. It would also incidentally put all the navigable streams of the West in direct connection for internal traffic, with the rivers of the States of Mississippi, Alabama and Georgia, which flow into the gulf of Mexico, and into the Atlantic from the St. John's to the Savannah rivers.

When steamers can take in their cargoes from the elevators at St. Louis, Cincinnati, Louisville and Memphis, or from the highest points of navigation in the West, and bring them, without breaking bulk, to European and Northern shipping on the Atlantic seaboard, or take them direct to the interior of the cotton, sugar and rice growing States of Mississippi, Alabama, Florida and Georgia, the value of such a work could scarcely be estimated; and when, by such an improvement, the two great producing sections of our country become united in all the departments of productive industry, they will spring forward with a power and energy but little dreamed of now, even by the most earnest and hopeful believers in the future progress and prosperity of these rich and fertile regions.

Besides uniting all the navigable streams of the West and South, for domestic traffic, and giving them a common outlet to two or more of the best harbors on the Atlantic coast, the construction of this inland water way would develop a source of national wealth that, without it, must to a great extent remain valueless.

Through a distance of 500 miles, from Pearl river in Mississippi to the Atlantic seaboard, there is an unbroken body of the best yellow pine timber in the world. The average width of this pine and live oak belt is not less than 150 miles; and through which, flowing into the bays and inlets which would form part of the channel, are innumerable small streams to bring to it the varied productions of this immense forest, not only to supply the increasing want of timber in the West, as well as foreign demand, but to furnish also an inexhaustible supply of the cheapest and best fuel for steamers engaged in its trade. The enhanced value of this extensive timber region, 75,000 square miles, made accessible by such an outlet would alone compensate for the cost of the work.

Water transportation, even when created by large expenditure of capital and labor, is so much less costly than transportation by rail, that heavy and bulky freight will follow the water. As a practical evidence of this fact, it is only necessary to observe the channels taken by the great bulk of commerce where the two modes are brought side by side in competition. Of the trade between the West and Northern Atlantic cities, the Erie canal, 350 miles long, carries over its elevation of 700 feet, and through its 80 locks, more than all the great trunk lines of railway between the St. Lawrence and Potomac rivers; and while it carries to New York more tonnage than all the foreign commerce of that city together. Its capacity in consequence of the growing demand for water transportation, is found insufficient, and it is now proposed to increase its dimensions so as to float vessels of 1,000 tons. It was originally built for boats of only 60 tons.

As great, however, as the trade through the Erie canal now is, or may be made by its enlargement, it could not equal that which would eventually flow through so capacious and lockless a channel as can be made from the Mississippi river to the Atlantic seaboard of the South. With this constructed water road (mapped out and more than half finished by nature) nearly 30,000 miles of inland steamboat navigation would come together and unite in one common highway to the ocean; producing a concentration of commercial resources unattainable in any other section of the world from one connected system of river transportation, and, as elsewhere, "the greatest commercial cities are those most advantageously situated with regard to the outlets, natural or artificial, of extensive river basins, and producing regions," so would this build up, at its Atlantic terminus on the Southern coast, a commercial center that could have no rival on the American continent; one that would become, by the controlling influence of cheap and safe transportation and geographical position, the gathering point of all the leading commercial staples of the United States, and as a consequence draw thither the great bulk of the trade of Europe, the West Indies and South America.

The agricultural and manufacturing interest of the South would keep pace with the growth of the great metropolis, which such a concentration of exchanges would build up; every eligible manufacturing locality and iron and coal mining district would at once be brought into requisition, and quadruple the business of all the railroad lines leading towards the Gulf and Southern Atlantic shore; and while these advantages would accrue to the South, by the construction of such an outlet, the industrial and commercial interests of the West would be no less benefited, their steamers and barge lines could pass within three days from the Mississippi river to the sides of ships of the largest tonnage, in the harbors of Fernandina, Brunswick, Savannah and Port Royal, within sight of that great "river in the sea" whose favoring currents insure prosperous voyages to all the markets of the world.

In regard to economy of construction, no other contemplated water way, from the Mississippi to the Atlantic ocean, is comparable with this gulf shore and peninsular route, and certainly none so available for a canal of sufficient capacity to admit the quick and uninterrupted passage of steamboats and barge lines engaged in the Mississippi river trade, and when surveys and estimates come to be made, by competent engineers, the wonder will be how easily and inexpensively such a work may be constructed.

Compared with the gulf passage, the navigation through this inland water road from the granaries of the West to Atlantic harbors, and European markets, would be shortened more than 800 miles, and of course subject to none of the dangers incident to a voyage around the reefs and capes of Florida, thus annually saving to the Western producers in the way of insurance alone, largely more than would pay the interest on the capital that would be required to construct all the connecting canals 200 feet wide and 6 feet deep, that would be requisite to form a continuous inland channel from the Mississippi river to the Atlantic seaports of Florida, Georgia and South Carolina.

Respectfully,
P. H. RAIFORD.

In conclusion the Committee would refer to the accompanying map (to be found in the front of this report), compiled by Col. RAIFORD, to illustrate the proposed route as recommended by the Committee.

All of which is respectfully submitted.

JAMES M. WILLIAMSON, Chairman.

The report was unanimously adopted.

The Chair announced the following special committees:

ON A SETTLED POLICY IN THE PUBLIC INTEREST IN REGARD TO THE DISPOSITION OF THE GOVERNMENT LANDS.—R. M Bishop, of Ohio; N. P. Banks, of Massachusetts, and W. I. Sykes, of Tennessee.

CONTINUOUS WATER LINE COMMUNICATION FROM THE MISSISSIPPI RIVER TO THE ATLANTIC OCEAN.—P. H. Raiford, of Florida; C. G. Forshey, of Texas, and T. N. Monroe, of Iowa.

(Under resolution of Mr. BOWMAN, of Kentucky.)

EDUCATION.—J. B. Bowman, Kentucky; R. C. Holliday, Maryland; R. M. Bishop, Ohio; W. M. Burwell, Louisiana, and J. M. Tibbetts, Arkansas.

Mr. ABLE, of Missouri, by unanimous consent, offered the following, which was unanimously adopted by a rising vote:

Resolved, That for the generous hearted hospitality so universally extended to us by the people of Cincinnati, we return them our most cordial thanks, and will bear with us to our homes, the lasting impression, that this is a city in which there lives a genuine appreciation of the efforts for the promotion of the commercial interests of the country, and that we leave with its citizens our most earnest wishes, that of our labors they may largely profit, and that their further prosperity may be as boundless as has been their liberality.

Mr. COLE, of Tennessee, presented and read the report of the Committee on Railways Generally, as follows:

The Special Committee on Railroads generally, respectfully submit the following report:

The subject referred to them is so comprehensive when considered in connection with the importance and magnitude of the interests involved, that it was found impossible for your committee, during the short time allowed them, to properly consider the numerous resolutions and suggestions relating to state and local improvements; and, not wishing to discriminate against any, it was deemed best not to refer to such local interests, and to confine the action of the Committee to questions of national importance.

In regard to railway management generally, the Committee respectfully recommend, that this Convention urges the importance of uniformity of gauge in the future construction of railroads.

Co-operation in railroad management has met with eminent success, and has given satisfaction to both the public and railway companies, wherever it has been fairly tested.

It is accordingly recommended, that all breaks and obstructions in our great highways of trade and travel be remedied, and the connection of tracks and uniformity of gauge be perfected as early as possible, so that trains may pass from one road to another, without annoyance or delay to either passengers or freight.

The Committee refer with pride to the fact, that the American continent is now crossed by a continuous line of rail, from the waters of the Atlantic, to those of the Pacific ocean, so that cars may run from Eastern cities to San Francisco, without the expense and damage attending the breaking of bulk in freight, or the change of cars by passengers.

Recognizing the railroad interests, as one of inestimable importance to the whole country, the Committee recommend that the Federal Government exercise the largest liberality toward these enterprises consistent with wholesome legislation, and especially those in the Southern States, which may have been crippled by the late unfortunate and deplorable war.

The Committee recommend the adoption of the following resolutions:

Resolved, That among the great enterprises proposed for the development of our whole country, the construction of a railroad connecting the waters of the Pacific ocean and the great lakes, by the Northern Pacific route, has the sympathy of this Convention.

Resolved, That expediency and justice alike demands, that the General Government should extend the same liberal aid to a Southern line of rail across the continent, as has been afforded the Northern Central for directly connecting the Northern States and railroad system with the oceans, on our Eastern and Western borders, as a measure in its impartial beneficence; tending at once, to give prosperity to our Southern Atlantic and gulf ports; vitalize the prostrated system of Southern railroads, stimulate production, and increase wealth in the entire interior South, and seal the affections of its people to the flag of the nation, and their devotion to the honor and best interests of the republic.

Resolved, That this Convention is opposed to any legislation that will unnecessarily obstruct, hinder and delay the passage across the rivers of our country, of railroads or other means of transit.

Resolved, That the policy adopted by many of the Southern railroads, in affording cheap transportation to persons seeking a settlement in the Southern States, or investigating and examining the resources of the same for the purpose of investment, is heartily approved by this Convention, as a measure well calculated to encourage immigration to those States.

Resolved, That this Convention recommend that Congress renew and extend the grants of alternate sections of land made to railroads in the South, which, after the initial construction of said roads, have lapsed in consequence of the interruption to all public enterprises, caused by the war.

Resolved, That the President of this Convention, be requested to furnish the President and Vice-President of the United States, and the Speaker of the House of Representatives, with a copy of the foregoing report and resolutions.

After some discussion, the report and resolutions were adopted, under a call for the previous question.

Mr. COLE, also presented the following supplemental report of the Committee:

The Special Committee on Railways Generally, beg leave to make the following additional report. That they earnestly recommend to this Convention, the following preamble and resolution:

WHEREAS, The State of North Carolina ceded to the United States, the territory now forming the State of Tennessee, an area of land surpassing in excellence and richness that derived from any other source, except the North-west Territory, ceded by Virginia; and

WHEREAS, One of the great highways from the Southern Pacific Railroad to the middle East, lies through her mountain lands; therefore

Resolved, That we recommend the passage by the United States Congress, of a liberal appropriation to the Trans-Atlantic Western North Carolina Railroad, and recommend its favorable consideration.

Which was adopted.

Mr. ABLE, of Missouri: Mr. Chairman, I call for the special order set for 11 o'clock, to-day.

The CHAIR: Before proceeding with the special order, a communication from the President of the United States will be read. (Applause.)

The Secretary read the following:

THEODORE COOK, *President Committee of Arrangements,*
Southern Commercial Convention:

DEAR SIR: I am in receipt of your letter inviting me to attend the sittings of the Southern Commercial Convention, to be held in Cincinnati during the present month.

It would afford me great pleasure to be able to be present, but my public duties will not permit me to leave the Capital at this time.

I earnestly hope the Convention may be successful in the object of its meeting, and that the interests of commerce may be greatly benefited by its deliberations.

I am, sir, very respectfully yours,
U. S. GRANT.

EXECUTIVE MANSION, Washington, D. C., October 4, 1870.

The Chair announced the following Special Committee on memorializing Congress to aid in the construction of a Southern Pacific Railroad:

S. W. Morton, Kentucky; George Throckmorton, Texas; V. A.

Gaskell, Georgia; J. B. Bowman, Kentucky; W. G. Brien, Tennessee; W. M. Burwell, Louisiana; R. M. Bishop, Ohio; John H. Kennard, Louisiana; C. A. Foster, Mississippi.

Mr. Cook: Gentlemen of the Convention, I expect with this to conclude my announcements to the Convention, which I have been from time to time making here. I want to announce to you, that at 2 o'clock, precisely, we propose to make a little excursion into the suburbs of the city. Carriages will be in attendance at head-quarters, at the Burnet House, and we expect all the delegates to go with us on this excursion. It is expected we shall make a halt at the residence of one of our hospitable citizens a little out of the city, and return by 6 o'clock. (Cheers.)

The special order set for 11 o'clock, A. M., was then announced, it being the resolution of Mr. J. B. Bowman, as follows:

Whereas, The Southern Commercial Convention, now in session, by its liberal policy and comprehensive action, has invited and secured a representation of the various commercial and industrial interests of the whole country, and has thereby assumed a national character and importance; therefore, be it

Resolved, That when this Convention adjourns, it will meet at ————, on ———— day, 1871, under the name and style of the "National Commercial Convention."

After some discussion, under a call for the previous question, on motion of Mr. Brien, of Tennessee, the resolution was unanimously adopted.

Mr. Dodge, of Arkansas, by unanimous consent, offered the following:

Resolved, That this Convention does cordially and most respectfully tender its thanks, to the Hon. John W. Garrett, for the able, dignified and impartial manner, in which he has discharged the arduous duties of presiding officer of this Convention.

On motion of Mr. Corwine, of Ohio, the resolution was amended by adding the words, "and to the other officers of the Convention, for the faithful discharge of their respective duties."

The resolution, as thus amended, was unanimously passed.

Mr. DODGE, of Arkansas, offered the following:

Resolved, That the thanks of this Convention are due, and are hereby heartily tendered to the various railroad lines, which have so generously tendered their courtesies to the returning delegates of this Convention.

Which was unanimously adopted.

Mr. OVERALL, of Mississippi, offered the following:

Resolved, That the press of Cincinnati, are entitled to the thanks of this Convention, for the able reports which have been made in extenso of the proceedings of this Convention.

Which was unanimously adopted.

Mr. SNYDER, of Tennessee, presented and read the report of the Committee on Central Line of Water Communication, as follows:

The Committee on a Central Line of Water Communication between the North and South, in view of the magnitude and importance of the subject referred to them, and of the time necessary to make a full investigation, and to present the proper estimates and statistics, beg leave of this Convention for said Committee to make their final report to the next Convention.

Which was adopted.

Mr. FORSHEY, of Texas, presented and read the report of the Committee on Trans-latitudinal Railroads, as follows:

The Special Committee on trans-latitudinal Railroads in the United States, beg leave to make the following report:

The Committee find,

1. That the patronage of the General Government has been invoked, and often granted to the construction of railroads lying chiefly along the parallels, or from East to West, while the same has rarely, and very moderately been granted to those which cross the latitudes, North and South.

2. That the demands of commerce are chiefly trans-latitudinal; calling mainly for exchange of unlike commodities and productions, which grow and are produced in diverse climates: for travel, from rigorous to more genial climates, or from fervid to torrid regions in summer, toward the cooler airs and more elevated countries North.

3. That there still remain great routes where these demands of commerce have not been able to effect a transit in consequence of mountain barriers, or unpeopled areas; and which call with equal justice for national aid, in their development with those enterprises to which great aid has been granted; therefore,

Be it resolved, 1st. That the great through routes, or important links in the same, tending North and South, be placed on the same footing as the lines along the parallels; and that the Congress of the United States be memorialized by this Convention, to give them equal aid and subsidy.

2d. In view of the foregoing premises, we commend to Congress a grant of such lands and monies, or mail subsidies, as may seem just and equitable, whenever they may be organized upon proper basis

1. To a line of railroad from Buffalo to Dunkirk, on the lakes, by Pittsburg to Charleston, on the Atlantic.

2. From Saginaw or Detroit, by Cincinnati to Savannah, and Brunswick and Apalachicola.

3. From Chicago or Michigan City, by way of Louisville, to Pensacola and Mobile.

4. From Marquette or Ontonagan, on lake Superior, by Cairo and Memphis, to New Orleans.

5. From St. Pauls or lake Itasca, by way of Kansas City, or Leavenworth City, mouth of Canadian and Tyler, to Galveston; and

6. From the North Pacific Railroad, along the 98th meridian, to Austin and San Antonio, and to Aransas and Corpus Christi bays, and the Rio Grande, in South-western Texas.

And also, from the Mississippi river, at or near the center of its course, the mouth of the Ohio, diagonally across the latitudes, through Little Rock and Austin, to the Rio Grande in such direction as to point to Mazatlan or San Blas, on the Pacific coast; and

WHEREAS, Most of these lines are largely advanced in construction, and need but little aid, the first and last three only, traversing portions of country but feebly populated, or unable to force themselves through.

3d. That we specially commend to the United States Congress, for such aid as may be just and equitable, the Galveston & Great Northern, and the International Companies, and whenever the population of the West shall justify it, the route near the 98th meridian.

All of which is most respectfully submitted.

The Committee further beg leave to submit the following preamble and resolutions, for adoption by the Convention:

WHEREAS, Two great lines of railway already traverse the great plains lying between meridian 95, and the Rocky mountains—the Kansas Pacific Railway from Kansas City, via Denver Pacific Railway, to Cheyenne, and the Union Pacific Railroad from Omaha, via Cheyenne, to Ogden—each connecting on the East and West with other lines, and connecting the East and West coasts of the continent; and

WHEREAS, These great railway lines are promoting the Westward extension of settlements on the great plains, and the promise is that at an early day there will be continuous lines of population across the region heretofore regarded as a treeless waste, unfitted for civilized uses, except for pastoral industry, to a limited extent; and

WHEREAS, The result of experiment shows that the grains and grasses essential to agricultural life, may be produced even without irrigation in many parts of the plains, heretofore regarded as too arid in climate, if not too sterile in soil for use in sustaining the vegitation of the farm; and

WHEREAS, The redemption of the great plains to civilized uses, is only practicable by the aid of railways; therefore, be it

Resolved, That the grants of lands to the Union Pacific, the Denver Pacific, and the Kansas Pacific Railways, have, in the opinion of this Convention, already been productive of beneficial results, not only in sustaining settlements on portions of the great plains, but also in enabling the people of that nutalliferous regions in the Territories and States of the West, to extend civilized industry, greatly to the advantage of their own and other industrial interests of the American people. And that the wisdom of the policy of granting aid to the aforesaid railways, is amply vindicated by its results.

Resolved, That this Convention respectfully represents to the Congress of the United States, that the public interests would be greatly subserved by a liberal grant of lands to secure the construction of a branch Pacific Railway, leaving the line of the Kansas Pacific Railway at some point not East of the 97th Meridian of longitude, and striking the line of the Atlantic & Pacific Railway, at some point East of Albuquerque in New Mexico. That such branch railway would prove of great use to the Government in military and postal service; would accommodate a large commerce of New Mexico, Arizona and Chihuahua; would afford additional facilities in developing the mineral and other resources of the interior mountain regions, and would greatly aid in redeeming the Western portion of the great plains to civilized uses.

Under a call for the previous question, the report and accompanying resolutions were adopted.

The Committee upon Railway Communications of the Cities of Virginia with the Great West, reported as follows:

Resolved, That the Special Committee upon the Railway connections of the Cities of Virginia with the Great West, be allowed to prepare their report, and present the same to the Convention at its next session. The said report, when prepared, may be published, if approved by a majority of the Committee.

Which was adopted.

Mr. Fox, of Nevada, offered the following :

Resolved, That this Convention would recommend for consideration at its session in 1871, the development of our gold and silver mines, in the Pacific States and Territories.

Which was adopted.

Mr. JAMES, of Tennessee, offered the following:

Resolved, That the cordial thanks of this Convention, be extended to Gov. N. P. BANKS, the acting Vice-President of the Convention, for his able and efficient support of the President in his laborious duties.

Which was unanimously adopted.

Gen. BANKS: Mr. Chairman, I take this opportunity, although I know the moments of the Convention are precious, of expressing my thanks for the resolution which has just been presented to this Convention.

1 confess, sir, that I came from Massachusetts to attend this Convention with some reluctance, because its character was not wholly understood by myself, and I have no doubt its scope is not thoroughly understood by very many of my fellow citizens in the more northern States of the Union.

I am glad to perceive here the wide views, generous concessions and spirit of kind feeling and cordiality which have been exhibited throughout the sittings of this Convention. I have said before, and

I know full well, the influence of this Convention will be marked very visibly.

I am glad of the opportunity of witnessing what I have seen here during the progress of the deliberations of this Convention, and I assure you, gentlemen, I shall lose no opportunity, wherever I shall be, of speaking in its praise and in its behalf. (Cheers.)

Although the State of Massachusetts is represented in this Convention by only one delegate, I do not doubt that, at the session which is to be held next year, you will find every State, and especially that part of the country least represented now, fully represented by its best men, without distinction of party, and without reference to personal interests. (Cheers.)

The great controversy through which we have passed, sir, was initiated outside of party, outside of parties; and the Union which is to follow that controversy, and which will make separation forever after impossible, will be initiated and carried through outside of political organizations. (Cheers.)

And those great interests, which represent the great material affairs of the country, which touch every man's pocket, and appeal to every man's heart, can best be controlled by conventions such as this. Those parties are the best that can do the most to seal the past, so far as the misfortunes of the country are concerned, in oblivion, by opening wide the heart and accepting all pledges in the spirit in which they are given, thus securing the prosperity of the country hereafter. (Cheers.)

Had I been present, I should have added my voice to that of the Convention, in honor of the presiding officer. But I desire to say now, sir, for myself and for those I have the honor to represent, at home, that we concur most cordially in the complimentary and well deserved expression of opinion which was unanimously adopted by the Convention. (Cheers.)

Mr. NEWMAN, of Georgia, offered the following:

Resolved, That to Mr. THEODORE COOK, the very efficient Chairman, and to the Committee of Arrangements, for the reception and entertainment of this Convention, the thanks of this Convention are due and the same are hereby unanimously tendered.

Adopted.

Mr. OVERALL, of Mississippi, offered the following:

Resolved, That the thanks of this Convention be tendered to managers of theaters for courteous attentions to members in providing for their entertainment.

Adopted.

Mr. WRIGHTSON, of Kentucky : Mr Chairman, I gave notice yesterday that I should move to reconsider a subject which was laid upon the table by a vote of this Convention. The subject was in reference to chartering a continuous line of railroad, from Norfolk, Virginia, to St. Louis, Missouri, by the Congress of the United States, by the way of the city of Louisville. I made the motion to lay upon the table, and I now move to reconsider the vote by which that subject was then laid upon the table.

After a lengthy discussion, the motion to reconsider prevailed.

The question being upon the adoption of the resolution as reported by the Committee on Ample Railroad Facilities from the Ohio River to the Central South, it was carried by a vote of 45 ayes to 35 nays.

Mr. SNYDER, of Tennessee, presented and read the report of the Special Committee on the Time and Place of Holding the next Convention; as follows :

The Committee appointed to select the place and designate the time for the meeting of the next Commercial Convention have the honor to report that Baltimore has been agreed upon as the place where, and the first Monday of October, 1871, as the time when, the next Convention shall meet.

Your Committee submit the following as the basis of representation for the next Convention :

Each incorporated city shall be entitled to one delegate, and to one additional delegate to every ten thousand inhabitants over the first ten thousand, provided that no city shall be entitled to more than ten delegates.

Each Territory, and the District of Columbia, shall be entitled to one delegate; and each State to one delegate for each Congressional district, to be appointed by the Governor.

Each incorporated railroad, steamboat, manufacturing and mining company in actual operation, having a cash capital of $100,000, shall be entitled to one delegate.

Every Chamber of Commerce and Board of Trade shall be entitled to one delegate.

The Committee of Arrangements shall have authority to invite persons of eminence in the arts and sciences, or in commercial and agricultural pursuits, and such other persons of distinction as they may deem to the interest of the Convention.

All of which is respectfully submitted.

On motion of Mr. PENDERY, of Arkansas, the report was amended by substituting for "the first Monday of October," the "third Monday of September," as the time for holding the next Convention.

The report as thus amended was adopted.

Mr. WICKERSHAM, of Alabama, offered the following:

Resolved, That a Committee of five be appointed by the Chair to memorialize Congress, at its next session, to open the canal around the Muscle shoals on the Tennessee river.

Adopted.

Mr. CLARK, of Alabama, offered the following:

Resolved, That the thanks of this Convention are hereby tendered to the fair ladies who have graced this Convention by their presence in the galleries during its sessions.

Adopted.

Mr. E. A. JAMES, of Tennessee, offered the following:

Resolved, That the Committees appointed by this Convention that fail to report to this Convention upon the various subjects referred to them, are requested to report to the next Convention the result of their labors.

Which was adopted.

Mr. KEENE, of Maryland, offered the following:

Resolved, That this Convention call the attention of governors of States, presidents of immigration societies, manufacturers and capitalists, willing to embark in industrial pursuits, to the thousands of skilled German artists and mechanics expelled from France in consequence of the present war raging between Germany and France, and request them to use all means in their power, and if necessary to advance material aid, to encourage them to come to the United States of North America with the assurance of a heartfelt welcome.

Resolved, That this Convention ask the aid of the Press of this country to give the largest publication to this subject, in order to bring it to the notice of all interested.

Which was adopted.

Mr. MACCABE of Arkansas, offered the following:

WHEREAS, By acts of Congress, approved July 4, 1866, certain lands were granted to the States of Missouri and Arkansas, for the purpose of extending the Iron Mountain Railroad from Pilot Knob, Missouri, to Helena, Arkansas; and

WHEREAS, The time in which the conditions precedent to the accruing of said grant of lands expires by limitation, in July, 1871; and

WHEREAS, It was impossible for the people of the State of Arkansas, to comply with said conditions since the passage of the act in 1866; and

WHEREAS, The State of Mississippi has chartered a railroad entitled the Mobile & Great North-western Railroad, running from Mobile, Alabama, to a point opposite Helena, in the State of Mississippi, which road will be a continuation of the Iron Mountain Railroad, constituting a great North and South trunk line from St. Louis to the gulf of Mexico; therefore

Resolved, That in view of the interest involved, and the importance of the projected railroad, this Convention respectfully recommend to to the United States Congress, an extension of the time in which to perform the conditions of the grant of lands limited in the act of Congress of July 1866.

Adopted.

Gov. FLETCHER, of Missouri: Mr. President, I move that this Convention now adjourn, to meet at Baltimore, on the third Monday of September, 1871.

Pending the motion to adjourn, Hon. John W. GARRETT, President of the Convention, made the following remarks:

Before submiting the motion to adjourn, the Chairman desires to return his profound acknowledgments to every member of the Convention for the co-operation, courtesy, and aid extended to him in the performance of his duties throughout its entire proceedings.

Rarely has so interesting a conference occurred—rarely, on any occasion, has so much good been effected in so limited a time. The cordiality and earnestness and fraternity which have been evinced by every delegate can not fail to have favorable reactive effects upon the entire country. (Cheers.)

Not one word of personal antagonism or criticism of an unkindly character has been uttered during the protracted deliberations, on so many and such important subjects. (Cheers.)

Why has this been the case, gentlemen? Because you have met as citizens of our common country, to deliberate upon our common interests, irrespective of any party relations (cheers) or demands, and thus the very hearts of the people—their true disposition, tone and sentiment have been developed. (Cheers.) Can it be otherwise, when we see such fraternity under such circumstances—when those who were engaged in the Confederate army meet those who served in the Federal army—those from the South meet on the soil of Ohio, citizens of the North, East and West, and combine in efforts for the common interests in perfect accord—can it be possible that, throughout the country, such expression, free from every political excitement, will not be recognized as exhibiting the real wishes of the people? (Cheers.)

I beg on behalf of the citizens of Baltimore, and of the State of Maryland, whom I have the honor to represent, to thank this Convention for selecting that city as the place for its next meeting, and I render this acknowledgment, not from ordinary motives, but because this action gives the assurance, in connection with the national character of the organization, that Maryland shall have the privilege, for which our people have longed since the close of the war, to show the whole country how perfectly, how honestly, in what a spirit of kindness they regard their Southern brethren, and to express that warmth and cordiality in personal intercourse. (Cheers.) I trust, gentlemen, that every member may return safely and happily to his home; that all may leave this beautiful and hospitable city, this splendid seat of commerce, full of pleasant memories; and that we may meet every member, with those who will be added to our number, in Baltimore, on the day proposed for the meeting of the next Convention. (Prolonged cheers.)

The motion is to adjourn this Convention to meet in Baltimore, on the third Monday in September next.

A delegate from Michigan, obtained the floor by the general consent of the Convention, and said:

Mr. Chairman, I desire to say that I had prepared a resolution which I had intended to offer, had opportunity presented itself, designating the city of Detroit for the place of holding the next Convention. As a member of the municipal government of that city, I wish to say, that had Detroit been selected as the place for holding the next Convention, nothing would have been wanting that could have been done on the part of the city. I would now like to offer a substitute, that the city of Detroit be designated by this Convention, as the next place of meeting, instead of the city of Baltimore.

Mr. ELLIOTT, of Tennessee: Mr. Chairman, five years ago, the first meeting of the National Board of Trade was held in the city of Detroit. That city, then sir, by her hospitality, her magnificence, and her liberality in the entertainment of the delegates, so covered herself over with glory, that there is not a spot left for that purpose, big enough to put your hand upon. (Much laughter.)

The motion of Gov. FLETCHER, to adjourn, was then put, and the Convention

ADJOURNED.

APPENDIX.

BANQUET.

At the invitation of the municipal authorities of the city of Cincinnati, extended through the Committee of Arrangements for holding the Convention, the delegates to the Southern Commercial Convention attended a Banquet given in their honor, on Friday evening, October 7th, 1870, in Pike's Music Hall. THEODORE COOK, Chairman of the Committee, presided, and JAMES F. TORRENCE served as Vice President. The delegates assembled in the rotunda of the Burnet House, at $7\frac{1}{2}$ o'clock, P. M., and after some time spent in general conversation they proceeded in a body to the Hall, being welcomed with music by Currier's Cornet Band. The Hall was profusely and appropriately decorated, the chief feature being the display of plants and flowers. The balcony was reserved for ladies who attended in evening dress. Covers for five hundred guests were provided. Two dais tables extended across the stage, at which were seated the President of the Banquet, with Hon. GEORGE H. PENDLETON on his right, and Judge H. C. WHITMAN on his left, the Vice Presidents of the Convention and invited guests. Six other tables extending from the Orchestra to the rear of the Hall accommodated the remainder of the guests. Tables were provided for journalists in the orchestra circle. Mr. COOK introduced the Rev. A. D. MAYO, who invoked Divine blessing upon the enjoyments of the evening. The delegates and guests were then seated and were served with the following:

BILL OF FARE.

SOUP.
Mock Turtle, - - Oyster.

FISH.
Salmon Mayonnaise, Lake Trout, Lobster Sauce.

BOILED.
Beef a la Mode, Boiled Chicken, Egg Sauce, Boiled Leg of Lamb, Caper Sauce.

ROAST.
Roast Turkey, Cranberry Sauce, Saddle of Mutton, Fillet of Beef, with Mushrooms.

ENTREES.
Sweetbreads, Tomato Sauce, Lamb Chops, French Peas, Croquettes de Volaille.

VEGETABLES.
Stewed Tomatoes, Sweet Potatoes, Stewed Corn, Green Peas.

OYSTERS.
Fried, - - - - - Raw.

GAME.
Prairie Chicken, Canvas-back Ducks, Quails, Larded.

COLD DISHES.
Westphalia Ham, Gelatine Turkey, Beef Tongue, Chicken Salad, Celery, Lobster Salad.

ORNAMENTS.
Of Natural Flowers, Candelabras, Grand Shell Composition, Charlottes, Nougat, Grand Meringues, Trees, Palmettoes, Parisian Vases, Mercantile Emblems made of Sugar, Ships, Railroads

PASTRY.
Cocoanut Pie, Lemon Pie, Cream Pie, Apple Pie, Custard Pie, Tarts.

CAKES.
Macaroons, Parisienne, Gateau, Fruit Cake, Wafer, Queen Cake, Jelly, Diamond Cake, Lady Fingers. Egg Kisses, Indian, Chocolate Cake, Seed Cake, Apcer, Almond Cake, Sponge, Cocoanut Drops, Silver Cake, Pound, &c.

DESSERT.
Pears, Apples, Raisins, Almonds, Hothouse Grapes, Concord Grapes, Catawba Grapes.

CONFECTIONERY.
Charlotte Russe, Burnt Almonds, Cream Candy, French Mottoes, Peppermint Drops, Caramels, Rose Mottoes, Plain Mottoes, Flower Mottoes, Snapping Mottoes, Fine-cut Mottoes.

ICE CREAM.
Vanilla, Chocolate, Richelieu, Lemon, Coffee, Strawberry, Pistachio, Cabinet.

ICES.
Lemon, Orange, Pineapple, Raspberry.

RELISHES.
Beets, Tomatoes, Pickles, Chow-chow, Olives, Catsup, Sauce, Horse-radish, Worcestershire, Cold Slaw.

JELLIES.
Maraschino, Orange, Rock Jelly, Bavarian, Madeira.

FRENCH COFFEES.

WINE LIST.
Catawba (still), Bogen's Diamond Sparkling, Ives' Seedling, Work's Golden Eagle, Champagne, Jules Mumm & Co., Dry Verzenay, Roederer's, Bouchefils & Co ; Whisky.

CIGARS.

SOUTHERN COMMERCIAL CONVENTION. 133

At 10 o'clock, President COOK arose and welcomed the delegates to the hospitalities of the evening, and announced the regular toasts in order as follows:

1st.— *Our Guests.*
Response by Judge H. C. WHITMAN, of Cincinnati.

2d.— *Agriculture.*
Response by Col. H. D. CAPERS, of Savannah, Ga.

3d.— *Commerce.*
Response by Gov. THOS. C. FLETCHER, of St. Louis, Mo.

4th— *Manufactures.*
Response by W. D. MOORE, Esq., of Pittsburg, Pa.

5th.— *Railroads.*
Response by R. S. ELLIOTT, Esq., of St. Louis, Mo.

[Hon. JOHN W. GARRETT, of Baltimore, Md., President of the Convention, was to have responded to the 5th toast, but was prevented in consequence of being summoned home by the death of a relative.—SEC.]

6th.— *River and Navigation Interests.*
Response by Hon. R. M. CORWINE, of Cincinnati.

7th.— *The United States.*
Response by Gen. NATHANIEL P. BANKS, of Massachusetts, who was received with rapturous and prolonged applause.

8th.— *Tennessee.*
Response by Hon. W. G. BRIEN, of Nashville, Tenn.

9th.— *Pennsylvania.*
Response by Gen. J. Z. SWEITZER, of Pittsburg, Pa.

10th.— *Virginia.*
Response by ISAAC H. CARRINGTON, Esq., of Richmond, Va.

11th.— *New York.*
Response by BENJ. P. BAKER, Esq., of New York city.

12th.— *Georgia.*
Response by Dr. E. S. RAY, of Atlanta, Ga.

13th.— *Kentucky.*
Response by Gen. GEO. W. CHILTON, of Louisville, Ky.

14th.— *Ohio.*
Response by Judge CHARLES R. RHODES, of Marietta, O.

15th.— *South Carolina.*
Response by J. BARRETT COHEN, Esq., of Charleston, S. C.

16th.— *Iowa.*
Response by T. M. MONROE, Esq , of Dubuque, Iowa.

17th.— *Mississippi.*
Response by Col. J. P. PRYOR, of Corinth, Miss.

18th.— *Louisiana.*
Response by Judge WM. M. BURWELL, of New Orleans, La.

19th.— *North Carolina.*
Response by J. C. MILLS, Esq., of Charlotte, N. C.

20th.— *Michigan.*
Response by Hon. RICHARD HAWLEY, of Detroit, Mich.

21st.— *Alabama.*
Response by Col. M. D. WICKERSHAM, of Mobile, Ala.

22d.— *Indiana.*
Response by Dr. W. S. PIERCE, of Indianapolis, Ind.

23d.— *Texas.*
Response by Gov. G. W. THROCKMORTON, of Austin, Texas.

24th.— *Nevada.*
Response by JOHN G. FOX, Esq., of Carson City, Nevada.

25th.— *Missouri.*
Response by Capt. BART. ABLE, of St. Louis, Mo.

26th.— *Maryland.*
Response by THOS. J. MCKAIG, Jr., Esq., of Baltimore, Md.

27th.— *Kansas.*
Response by Judge J. L. PENDERY, of Leavenworth, Kansas.

28th.— *Florida.*
Response by Dr. R. B. BURROUGHS, of Tallahassee, Fla.

29th.— *Massachusetts.*
Response by Gen. N. P. BANKS, of Mass.

30th.— *Illinois.*
Response by

31st.— *Wisconsin.*
Response by

At the conclusion of the responses, Mr. THEODORE COOK, was loudly called for, and after he had responded with a few well timed remarks, the banquet concluded at 2½ o'clock, A. M.